Bob Marley

THE STORIES BEHIND EVERY SONG

THIS IS A CARLTON BOOK

This edition published by Carlton Books Limited 2011

Text and design copyright © Carlton Books Limited 1998, 2011

A CIP catalogue for this book is available from the British Library

ISBN 978-1-84732-778-9

Printed in China

The publishers would like to thank the following sources for their kind permission to
reproduce the pictures in this book.

Bridgeman Art Library: 153
Corbis: /Bettmann: 99, 120, 128, 134, 142, 152; /Bettmann/UPI: 117; /Bojan Breolj:
88; /David Cumming/Eye Ubiquitous: 84; /Howard Davies: 7; /Lyn Goldsmith: 65, 123,
138; /Daniel Laine: 16, 114, 147; /Tim Page: 104; /Neal Preston: 56, 139; /UPI: 13
Getty Images: 127; /Paul Bergen/Redferns: 109; /Ian Dickson/Redferns: 5b, 67; /Dave
Ellis/Redferns: 59; /John Kirk/Redferns: 26; /Keith Morris/Redferns: 163; /Michael Ochs
Archives/Redferns: 8, 31, 37; /David Redfern: 19; /Ebet Roberts/Redferns: 51, 144, 157;
/Gai Terrell/Redferns: 165; /Charlyn Zlotnik/Redferns: 93
London Features International: 40, 47, 66, 69, 97; /Paul Cox: 53; /Mick Prior: 38
Panos Pictures: /Marc French: 149
Peter Simon Photography: 6, 10, 17, 21, 25, 30, 33, 46, 57, 73, 79, 95, 103, 106,
124, 135, 146, 167
Pictorial Press: 112; /Van Houten: 87
Retna Ltd: 5t; /Adrian Boot: 22, 125; /David Corio: 94, 140; /Chris Craske: 154; /Jill
Furmanovsky: 74, 133; /Gary Gershoff: 72; /Youri Lenquette: 29, 92; /Michael Putland:
48, 60, 100
Dave Saunders: 80, 83, 130
Maureen Sheridan: 44
Topfoto.co.uk: 4, 34
Vin Mag Archive Ltd: 161

Every effort has been made to acknowledge correctly and contact the source and/
or copyright holder of each picture and Carlton Books Limited apologises for any
unintentional errors or omissions, which will be corrected in future editions of this book.

Bob Marley

THE STORIES BEHIND EVERY SONG

MAUREEN SHERIDAN

CARLTON
BOOKS

CONTENTS

BEGINNINGS

At first glance, Nine Miles, in St Ann, Jamaica, the birthplace of Bob Marley, is nothing out of the ordinary. But then look again, and listen closely for the "natural mystic" that really does run through the air, and this typical Jamaican village of brightly-painted, one-room board houses, perched on a hillside nine miles from nowhere, starts to feel different.

In 1944, Jamaica was still a colony, and Captain Norval Marley, a middle-aged white Jamaican of the British West India Regiment, was stationed in the parish of St Ann. Then, as now, a white man in rural Jamaica was a rarity and to young Cedella Malcolm, Captain (as she called him) cut a fine figure as he rode his horse around the area.

Captain Marley was well-liked by the villagers of Nine Miles, and had been a long-time friend of Cedella's father, Omeriah Malcolm. By Miss Marley's account, the short, slim, white soldier had had his eye on her for some time before seducing her when she was only 16 years old, in the small house that the Captain – who Cedella remembers as "very handsome, very loving, very sweet" – had been renting from her grandmother, YaYa.

Robert Nesta Marley was conceived one seemingly ordinary night in early May. "He told me he loved me and I believed he did," says Cedella of the Captain, who wed her in a short service held on her grandmother's veranda eight months before her baby's expected birth.

The day after the wedding, the Captain departed for Kingston, coming back to Nine Miles only a couple of times to see the "straight-nosed" mulatto baby boy who had been born on February 6, 1945, in the little house up on the hill that he had purchased for his young bride.

After a rather idyllic first few years in the never-ending children's playing-field that is rural Jamaica, Marley's father came back

BILLBOARD ON THE
ROAD TO OCHO RIOS.

into his life to take him, as is the norm for many Jamaicans, to boarding school in Kingston. A photograph taken shortly after he left home, shows the young, brown Marley boy with his hair in a very British side-parting, a visual reminder of the two very different cultures from which he had been created.

For several months after Nesta had left home, Cedella didn't hear a thing from either husband or son. Then, she recounts, an acquaintance saw the six-year-old playing on a Kingston street. Mrs Marley's trip to town to find Nesta resulted in her taking him back to the country, discovering him as she did, not at boarding school, but on the streets of downtown Kingston where he had been living with an old lady named Miss Grey. A year or so later, the young Marley would move back to town with his mother, a move very difficult for him at the time, but one which would prove critical to his destiny.

*"WHEN THE
ROOT IS STRONG,
THE FRUIT IS
SWEET."*
BOB MARLEY

As the john-crows fly, Nine Miles and Trench Town are a mere 80 miles apart, but worlds apart in culture and living conditions. Nesta had a hard time fitting in – "country come a town" say Jamaicans to sum up the shock. But, as childhood gave way to adolescence, Nesta began to grow comfortable with the ghetto ("too comfortable," his mother would later lament), where his friendship with two other country "bwoys" was about to give him one hell of a future.

KINGSTON 13

Around the time of the late Fifties and early Sixties, Jamaican music was just beginning to bubble. Opportunities to cut a tune for the ruling producers of the day abounded. Nesta Marley, and his longtime friend Neville Livingston (who later would become "Bunny Wailer"), along with other budding talents of the area like Desmond Dekker, teamed up together (while Marley's mother, Cedella, teamed up with "Taddy", Livingston's father) and started to get gigs in local bars with the intention of getting tight enough for the recording studio. But as Marley's dreams of a future in music grew stronger daily, his mother, in the way of many of her generation, was steering him towards a "real" job – welding.

Mrs Booker's version of this short-lived apprenticeship has it ending with Bob's eye injury on the job. Marley's own version has the eye injury happening to Desmond Dekker (who'd followed him to the welding yard). Either way, it was a fortuitous injury for both of them. As Marley told it: "The days him (Dekker) have off him check out Beverley's (production company) and him do 'Honour Thy Father And Mother'… a big hit in Jamaica. After that him say, 'come man'."

From the beginning, Chinese Jamaicans have had a strong hand in the island's pop music industry, and restauranteur, Leslie Kong, was one of the first "Chineys" to set up shop – naming his label "Beverley's" after the restaurant he operated, with his brother, in downtown Kingston (and which also served as a legal front for a Chinese numbers game). Kong was enticed into music production by a young and eager James Chambers (soon rechristened by Kong as Jimmy Cliff). Cliff, in turn, told his friends, including Desmond Dekker, about Kong. Marley, encouraged by Dekker, soon also found his way to Federal Records (Kong's production base) which was a mere couple of miles from Trench Town, and which Rita Marley would buy in 1985 and turn into Tuff Gong.

NATTY THREADS – BUNNY WAILER, BOB MARLEY AND PETER TOSH IN SLICK SUITS BOUGHT FOR THEM BY COXSONE DODD.

HOPE ROAD, THE PLACE OF BOB MARLEY'S BIRTH.

Neither Marley nor Kong ever saw their relationship as anything but business. In fact, when Kong died at 38, it was widely believed that his death was due not to a heart attack as officially reported, but to an "obeah" (voodoo) curse put on him by Bob for releasing an album – *The Best Of The Wailers* – without permission. As intriguing as this obeah story is, Bunny Wailer dismisses it angrily, as he dismisses other obeah rumours, as "an outright lie". What remains unchallenged, however, is the fact that Bob Marley didn't like Leslie Kong.

Unlike later producers of Marley's work like Coxsone Dodd and Lee "Scratch" Perry, Leslie Kong is not known for having a serious ear for music, nor did he have any technical capability in the studio. But even when relegated to the role of financial backer, Leslie Kong certainly had a feel for which artists to back. And Randall Grass, founder of Shanachie Records, has written of Kong's "ear for quality", noting that, contrary to popular opinion, he did have a signature sound.

Allowing that Kong lacked "Perry's depth" and "Dodd's innovation", Grass credits Kong – who would one day oversee the Paul Simon 'Mother And Child' Reunion sessions at Dynamic Studios – with "stripping the music down to gimmick-free formulaic essentials". And no one can deny Kong's instinct for business. He was the first investor in Chris Blackwell's Island Records, a risky but ultimately very profitable decision that, sadly, he never lived to enjoy.

"ME GREW UP IN THE COUNTRY, IN THE WOODS – TO THE CITY, YA KNOW. A PLACE NAMED ST ANN. THEY CALL IT THE GARDEN PARISH. AN' ME GROW IN KINGSTON AN' LIVE IN TRENCH TOWN FROM 1958 TO 1961." **BOB MARLEY**

'Judge Not', and the other song that was recorded at that first session, 'Do You Still Love Me?', were released both in Jamaica and Europe (the latter release, significantly, by Chris Blackwell whose fate would be so intertwined with Marley's) under the artist name, "Bob Morely" – the way many Jamaicans pronounce "Marley". Kong also tried to get Marley to change his name to "Bobby Martell" (à la Bobby Rydell), but although at least one record would go out under that pseudonym, it didn't stick.

Kong would produce five other tracks with Marley as a solo singer before Bob became a part of The Wailers, and temporarily parted company with his original producer reportedly for non-payment of recording fees owing to him for two tunes.

About the same time that Marley's mother gave up the constant battle for survival on Kingston's cold and calculating streets and began planning a move to the United States, he and Bunny Wailer linked up with fellow Trench Town teen, Peter McIntosh. Tosh (his abbreviation) was also a country boy. Born in the small fishing village of Belmont, Westmoreland, close to Negril, he moved to West Street in Trench Town from another Kingston address, when the aunt who had been his surrogate mother died (his real mother having given him up shortly after birth). Marley, Wailer and Tosh had known each other, and had been jamming together for a while – "we used to sit in the back of Trench Town and sing" – but only became a formal group (with Junior Braithwaite and two backing singers) when singer Joe Higgs, later hailed as the "Godfather of Reggae", started to take an interest in them.

"Higgs," said Marley, "taught me many things." And the reggae star's mentor doesn't mind being remembered most for being Bob Marley's teacher, as long as his own contribution to reggae is acknowledged. As he says, when the Fifties ended and the Sixties (a creative decade for music worldwide) began, Kingston's burgeoning population of musicians was sensing the birth of something that was, in Higgs' words, "a new era... where the music wouldn't be 'do-overs' (covers), but songs that we wrote ourselves". To assist in this development, Higgs, though he never intended to be a teacher, set up teaching shop in his Trench Town yard. His students included The Wailers. Higgs taught all three the "rudiments of music... pitch and harmony structure... I helped them with everything. It was difficult to get the group to be precise in their sound... it took a couple of years to get it perfect"

It was also Higgs who, along with percussionist Alvin "Seeco" Patterson, set The Wailers up with Clement "Coxsone" Dodd.

Dodd's role in the formative years of the island's music was critical. Reviled by some, because of a lingering reputation for ripping off a number of great, yet naïve, artists in the days when doing a tune for a "'ducer" – for a few pounds – was seen as fair exchange. Through his fabled Studio One, Dodd is also revered as the man most instrumental in turning the strong but scattered energy of Kingston's young music scene into a full-fledged, unstoppable force.

Dodd began producing after several years of owning "sets" – the travelling, open-air discos that have always played a critical role in the island's entertainment options, as well as being a prime vehicle for the exposure of new recording artists. These sets, or sound systems, travel with huge, 50,000-watt banks of speakers not only to city venues but also from town to town to give rural residents a trendy and cheap night out (admission runs from JA$50.00 to $100.00, roughly £1 to £2). Dodd, while not the first to operate such a system, is generally credited with fathering the modern form of this uniquely Jamaican phenomenon by creating the "selector", the man (there are still no women) who not only spins the records but who also "toasts" (raps) in between and over the rhythms. The best of these selectors have become dancehall stars in their own right. "I came up with the idea, with my DJ, that we should rap with the people," says Dodd. It was an idea that stuck.

From his involvement with the sound systems, Dodd notes that when rock'n'roll took over from R&B as the First World's cool music of choice, Jamaicans (who have never taken to rock) were ready for a new music form of their own. Astute entrepreneur that he was, Dodd seized on the opportunity to move into recording with artists like Ken Boothe, Alton Ellis, Toots And The Maytals, Burning Spear, The Soulettes (Rita Marley's group), and Marcia Griffiths (later to be one-third of the I-Threes, Marley's backing vocalists). In the process, he became one of the most influential, and certainly the most prolific, of Jamaican producers.

But Bob Marley, as Dodd saw it, was more than just another artist on the Studio One roster. "Bob was with me for about five years. He lived at the back of the studio (in a small room that Bob strongly believed to be haunted) and I sort of adopted him because his mother wasn't here." Dodd also admits to being the first to separate Bob from The Wailers (a significant switch for which Chris Blackwell would later be blamed), because he sensed that he "was the one". But the fact that along the way some titles were released as "Peter Tosh and The Wailers", suggests that it was more often just a case of who happened to be on lead vocals.

In The Wailers' first Studio One incarnation, the group included Junior Braithwaite, as well as Beverley Kelso and Cherry Smith, the two back-up singers. But this sextet was quickly pared down to what Bunny Wailer calls the "no baggage Wailers".

Jamaica in the early Sixties was in transition from a colony to an independent state. When the power shift came in 1962, it was marked on August 5 by a euphoric, midnight ceremony attended by HRH Princess Margaret – who would return to Jamaica in 1997, as a guest of Chris Blackwell, staying at the now Blackwell-owned Ian Fleming estate, GoldenEye – her then husband, the Earl of Snowden, and Lyndon Baines Johnson, vice president (to President John F Kennedy) of the United States. Independence brought with it a vitality that invigorated, albeit temporarily, all aspects of Jamaican life. Music especially benefited from this new free spirit, and it is no coincidence that the beginning of the nation's musical identity commenced with its severing of colonial ties.

Clement Coxsone Dodd, after signing The Wailers to a tight five-year production/management deal, scored a hit with their third Studio One recording, 'Simmer Down', a rollicking, ska survival anthem that featured a backing band made up of some of Jamaica's best musicians, including the internationally renowned trombonist, the late Don Drummond.

In the wake of this success, Dodd began to groom his group in earnest, outfitting them in the slim-fitting mohair and lame suits so favoured by the US R&B groups of the Fifties, and putting them on a £3 a week salary.

KINGSTON, JAMAICA, THE INDEPENDENCE CELEBRATIONS IN 1962 MARKED THE END OF 300 YEARS OF BRITISH RULE.

As the owner of several sound systems, Dodd was in the enviable position of having instant access to the public ear. Jamaican radio was, and remains, resistant to anything new or different, and without these outdoor sessions, much of this daring music emerging from the ghetto would never have been exposed. Dodd also used his sets to popularize his acts, sending them around the country to perform with his Downbeat set.

"THE ONLY TRUTH IS RASTAFARI." BOB MARLEY

1964 was a big year for the young Wailers. In February, 'Simmer Down' hit Number One, and the group was consistently in the charts for the rest of the year. Many of these first Wailers recordings have stood the test of considerable time, remarkable in light of the fact that when Dodd first opened Studio One (after first experimenting in production at Ken Khouri's Federal Records Studio), he only had a one-track tape machine bought from Federal when Khouri upgraded to a two-track. Dodd later purchased the two-track when Federal invested in an eight-track. And, like the output of most of his peers, Dodd's productions were almost all "one-take" – or, "run tune and done".

As Jamaican music took on a form of its own so did its religion. Rastafarianism, which first emerged in the early Thirties, began to spread rapidly becoming the religion of choice for the disenfranchised people of the shanty towns who were, in the first flush of the island's independence, more than ready for a new Messiah – especially a black one.

The Rasta movement, with its worship of Emperor Haile Selassie I of Ethiopia, based much of its philosophy on the back-to-Africa teachings of black orator and entrepreneur Marcus Mosiah Garvey (he formed the ill-fated Black Star Line, the name obviously a take-off on Cunard's mammoth White Star Line), who, like Marley, came from the parish of St Ann. However, it was not until Rasta and reggae music – which took over from ska and rocksteady – merged that the religion became such a powerful and influential phenomenon.

"The only truth is Rastafari;" said Marley, who would also describe his faith as "not a culture but a reality."

The reality of Rastafari was first shown to Marley while he was with Dodd. Many of Coxsone's musicians were already sprouting locks and sporting the red, green and gold African identity of the Rastaman. Peter Tosh and Bunny Wailer were similarly intrigued. Rastafari appealed most to the rebels in society, those who questioned the sociopolitical system. Besides, the teachings of Rasta couldn't be properly ingested without generous helpings of herb (all the better to meditate), a perk that gave Jah Rastafari a serious edge over the traditional church.

As it turned out, Rasta wouldn't just appeal to the blacks of the Diaspora for whom its message was originally intended, but also to the vast population of white "hippies" (or those of kindred mind) left over from the Sixties. The anti-system stance of Rastafari, coupled with its emphasis on natural living, and a world future of peace, love and unity was attractive enough, but add to that a little intoxicating sensimillia and a "killer riddim" and who could resist?

Having locksed and "trimmed" twice (at his mother's request) before making a final commitment to Rastafari when he came back to Jamaica from the US, Marley had mulled over his conversion for a long time in light of the "outlaw" status conferred on followers of the faith by the conservative majority of Jamaicans. But, once he had fully accepted Jah as "earth's rightful ruler", he quickly became the movement's most visible and powerful exponent – a role for which no successor has ever been found.

Saddened that he had been off the island during the April 1966 visit of Haile Selassie, a visit treasured by the Rastafarian community (despite the Emperor's vehement denials of divinity, and his brief panic attack when he saw the vast sea of welcoming dreadlocks), Marley began a significant association with Rasta elder Mortimer Planner shortly after his return from America. Planner would continue as Marley's spiritual adviser and friend for many years.

Bob's spiritual beliefs became more entrenched, and his focus changed from love songs to message music. Yet producers like Dodd, Kong and, later, American Danny Sims, shied away from recording the songs with serious lyrics. Sims especially wanted to keep Marley playing as much R&B mainstream as possible to penetrate the US market.

Danny Sims had met The Wailers in 1967, when he and singer Johnny Nash came to Kingston to record a new Nash album. The decision to produce in Jamaica had been made primarily to cut costs – Jamaican studio rates then being far cheaper than those of comparable international rooms – but Sims soon realized that the island was a place for good songs. He was especially impressed by Marley's writing and commissioned him to write songs for Nash, two of which, 'Stir It Up' and 'Guava Jelly', would become US pop hits. He also signed the three Wailers to a production and publishing deal with JAD Records and Cayman Publishing, putting them all on a modest living allowance of $100 a week each.

The Wailers recorded almost 90 songs for Sims, songs that would form the basis of the 1999 release, *The Complete Bob Marley 1967 to 1972*. Heralded by the international press as equal to "stumbling on

Picasso's complete Cubist works", in Jamaica, the collection was accorded customary, and slightly cynical, nonchalance.

The practice of releasing albums made up of various singles that The Wailers' first producers had recorded began early. Leslie Kong released *The Best Of The* Wailers (Beverley's), as did Dodd in two volumes (Studio One and Buddha), prompting a furious Marley to complain that "the best" hadn't happened yet. Both of these albums were then re-released under different titles, a devious practice that still hasn't ended.

Dodd also put out *The Wailing Wailers* (Studio One), *Marley, Tosh And Livingston* (Studio One), *The Birth Of A Legend* (Calla and CBS), *Early Music – Bob Marley And The Wailers featuring Peter Tosh* (CBS), and *Bob Marley And The Wailers with Peter Tosh* (Hallmark).

Danny Sims entered the picture later, releasing *Soul Rebel* (New Cross) before *Chances Are* (Cotillion).

*"TO THIS DAY,
THE ONLY LEGAL
WAY OUT OF
THE GHETTO
FOR MANY OF
ITS YOUT' IS
THROUGH THE
MUSIC."*
BOB MARLEY

JUDGE NOT

Auditioning this song *a cappella* for Kong, the teenaged Nesta Marley, while not earning the producer's praise, did impress enough for him to "get through" – Jamaican parlance for getting what you want: in this case, Bob Marley's first outing on wax. The year was 1961.

'Judge Not', a ska single released on Kong's Beverley's label didn't make much of a dent anywhere, and would have vanished without regret had its singer not had a destiny unimaginable at the time.

"It nevah really do nuttin', but it a good song still," said Marley when recalling his freshman recording effort after he became a major star.

Others were not as complimentary, citing the song's distinctive penny whistle as irritating.

Leslie Kong, whose biggest hit as a producer was Desmond Dekker's Seventies' smash, 'The Israelites' (which Jews the world over interpreted as being about them, when in fact it was an early call to the black "Diaspora"), recorded his artists at Federal Studio owned by Syrian, Ken Khouri, on Marcus Garvey Drive. Khouri, another Jamaican music pioneer was the first to offer (in 1954) recording and pressing at one location – a couple of decades later, Tuff Gong, Marley's own facility, would occupy premises and offer similar services after the complex was bought by his widow to house the manufacturing and distribution facilities formerly based on Hope Road.

The relationship between the producer and the artist was a tenuous one from the outset. As Bob himself told it: "I meet Leslie Kong at Federal... and that man rude. Tell me sing my song straight out standing outside... him tek me inna room, past Chinaman, and this guy (Ken Khouri) who tek the money... so I sang (and) say to him, 'what if it a hit?'... then man a name a Dowling mek me sign the release form dem, den push me outta studio."

BOB "FAMILY MAN" MARLEY.

There are conflicting reports of what Marley got paid for his first session. His mother remembers it as £5 out of which she got £2 ("he always made sure his Mama got her cut"), her sister, Enid, ten shillings, and a friend, five, leaving her son with £2.10 (the same amount as her weekly housekeeping wage). Don Taylor, who would later manage Marley, recounts it as £20, a figure that Bob himself confirmed by saying he got two £10 notes. Whatever the exact amount (and the arithmetic doesn't seem to add up entirely), Kong got a bargain.

'Judge Not'/'Do You Still Love Me?' was released internationally in 1963 in London by a young British-born white Jamaican, Christopher Blackwell, who, a decade later, released *Catch A Fire*, The Wailers first album on his own Island Records label, and who would be the man commonly credited with giving Bob Marley to the world.

I'M STILL WAITING

From a lyrical perspective, 'I'm Still Waiting' is not one of Bob Marley's best, but this song is significant in that it was recorded at the first Studio One session, along with 'It Hurts To Be Alone' (written and sung by Junior Braithwaite). The song is also significant for its beautiful, haunting vocal (once you get past the kitsch opening bars). Owing much to the harmony arrangements of popular R&B groups of the day, the production is original enough to hold the ear, and the emotion of the singer captures the listener over and over again. Some have speculated that the slight lag between singer and musicians was intentional, but with Coxsone's studio being a one-track facility, that would have been impossible. The more prosaic technical explanation, according to engineer Barry O'Hare, without knowing whose track was being analysed, is that the singer was behind the rhythm.

'I'm Still Waiting' was one of a string of hits that the group had in 1966, for which they each reportedly got only £60, angering Marley to the point where, before thinking better of it, he considered taking up a gun and "going down there to blast away. These (producers) put out 200 songs a year with 60 different labels and 900 different singers... Jamaicans go slow, everything is 'soon come', but if there's one thing Jamaicans rush about it's making a recordin'... them guys killer of reggae music." The sad thing about Marley's astute observations – made about 20 years ago – is that nothing, really, has changed.

SIMMER DOWN

The deceptively simple lyrics of 'Simmer Down', The Wailers' first Jamaican hit, are as relevant to the fires of discontent that burn in downtown Kingston today as they were when Bob Marley wrote the lyrics in the Sixties. "The battle (would) get hotter," he predicted with some accuracy.

Recorded for Coxsone Dodd, 'Simmer Down' spoke to the endemic social unrest of urban Jamaica as no other song before it. Many of the musicians on this Studio One session are now dead, and Dodd's Brentford Road studio, long out of vogue, was recently dismantled and the equipment advertised for sale. Ernie Ranglin, the guitarist and arranger of the song, spoke bitterly of the experience. "I don't remember anything about those times," he says. "I wanted to forget everything that happened... people made their money off it... let them remember." Dodd's session

"JAMAICANS GO SLOW, EVERYTHING IS SOON COME, BUT IF THERE'S ONE THING THEY RUSH ABOUT IT'S MAKING A RECORDIN'... THEM GUYS KILLER OF REGGAE MUSIC."
BOB MARLEY

ERNIE RANGLIN,
GUITARIST AND
ARRANGER ON
'SIMMER DOWN'.

musicians were paid a paltry £2 a tune, so perhaps Ranglin's regrets, in the light of the millions made from the song, aren't surprising.

'Simmer Down', first aired only hours after it was recorded on Dodd's sound system, was released on the Coxsone label just before Christmas in 1963, and was a bona fide Jamaican hit by February of the following year (even if, as myth has it, The Wailers had to personally go to the radio stations and threaten the DJs with death if they didn't play it – a more direct and less expensive method to ensure airplay than the more familiar "payola").

The first live rendition of the track, and supposedly the group's first public performance, was given at a talent show at the Majestic Theatre. The Wailers won over the traditionally tough Jamaican audience with what was described by singer Alton Ellis as this "different kind of music", but didn't win the contest – provoking what was later reported as an all-out brawl between Marley and the night's victors, the long-forgotten Uniques.

But the hit had its critics. As Bunny Wailer, downplaying the song's significance points out, the melody wasn't original and the track didn't earn The Wailers the respect of their peers. "It was a nursery rhyme song, something that people heard every day, a nursery rhyme that is sung in schoolyards, in back yards, but that was the record that hit. So… people didn't rate the record. They said to us you didn't do any record, don't take that for nuttin', you're lucky. You better make sure and record one we want to hear, some serious lyrics."

Nursery rhyme or not, 'Simmer Down' got The Wailers noticed. It also got them a regular recording gig with Dodd, who as well as advancing money for slick stage clothes, put the trio on a weekly wage of £3 each (recoupable of course). For the first time, The Wailers were living – if modestly – off their musical works.

PUT IT ON

This Coxsone Dodd-produced ska cut was played repeatedly at Bob and Rita's, humble – yet by the bride's account very happy – home wedding on February 10, 1966. On February 11 (like his father before him, who had left Marley's mother the day after their wedding) Marley left Rita for Delaware. The grainy black-and-white photo taken that day shows a young, happy and very ordinary couple, blissfully unaware that they were about to embark on a very extraordinary life.

The former Rita Anderson had met Bob in the lanes that led from Trench Town to Studio One on Brentford Road. The Wailers had to pass close to Rita's house (where she lived with her Aunt Viola) to get to the studio, and the nursing student-cum-singer (she had dreams, too), had wangled a meeting, getting to know the trio better when her vocal group, The Soulettes, made their way to Studio One. Although Rita, who was already the mother of one-year-old Sharon, had first gravitated towards Peter Tosh, she then switched focus to Bob (stirring, some say, the first

"ME COME BACK A JAMAICA AN' DO 'BEN' DOWN LOW", WHICH WAS A HIT AN' DEM ROB WE OUT OF IT AGAIN. WE COME BACK WITH 'NICE TIME', BUT MAN IS ALL ROBBERY… ROB YOU DOWN TO NUTTIN'."
BOB MARLEY

RITA MARLEY WITH
THE MARLEY KIDS.

jealousy between the two men). 'Put It On' was recorded during the couple's first months together, and thus was a fitting theme song to celebrate their marriage.

Bob's mother, in her book, *Bob Marley*, doesn't paint as sweet a picture of Bob's marriage which, she says, her son denied, putting the whole event down to the conjuring of a "Madda" (obeah woman) who kissed his hand, "and the next thing he knew he was married to Rita". Others, like Don Taylor, add to the speculation by reporting that Rita's Aunt Viola (who Bob was said to fear), was an obeah woman.

BEN' DOWN LOW

'Ben' Down Low' was a Number One in Jamaica, but they were "pressin' it, sellin' it… a black market type a business", said Marley of the song that reaped them no royalties and precipitated The Wailers' split with Dodd and Studio One. 'Ben' Down Low' was the first song produced after Marley's return to JA following one of his two brief working stints in middle America. "Me come back a Jamaica an' do 'Ben' Down Low', which was a hit an' dem rob we out of it again. We come back with 'Nice Time', but man is all robbery… rob you down to nuttin'."

A perfect dance tune, 'Ben' Down Low' neatly describes all Jamaican styles of dance from African-inspired folk to today's raunchy dancehall, but never was it used more effectively than in this catchy ska tune, which will still get any Jamaican over 40 on the dance-floor in seconds.

BOB, PETER AND BUNNY

THE INFAMOUS
LEE 'SCRATCH'
PERRY DEFINED THE
WAILERS' SOUND IN
THE STUDIO.

The next producer to enter the picture was Lee "Scratch" Perry. It was Perry who defined The Wailers' reggae sound, bringing out the bass as a lead instrument and pulling from Bob and the other Wailers, lead vocals that have an ethereal quality that could penetrate the hardest heart.

Everybody in Jamaican music has a Lee "Scratch" Perry tale to tell. There was the time he covered his Black Ark Studio (both inside and out) with tiny "X's" (it took several weeks); the time he appeared at a memorial concert for seminal reggae producer Jack Ruby, dressed in a red and white satin suit and hat, as *Alice In Wonderland's* Mad Hatter, with a very tall, buxom blonde on his arm; the time he was spotted outside Nassau's Compass Point Studio tuning the grey, static screen of a broken television "to outer space"; and the time he crushed a red brick to mud in his Bahamas bathroom and left it for a very unhappy maid to clean up. Debate about the authenticity of his madness continues and it's said that he once feigned madness to thwart gunmen who were after him, and then the hoax stuck. But, fact or fiction, no other individual, has added as many colourful stories to Kingston's musical lore as Perry.

Apart from being gossip-worthy, Perry is also very good at what he does. Chris Blackwell is one of a number of people who give Perry the credit for producing The Wailers' best material. This even though it was the music Blackwell had a hand in that broke the band internationally. "Lee Perry had an incredible feel," Blackwell says. "A kind of magic... Perry was one of the master music people I believe."

Perry began his production career with Coxsone Dodd as the Downbeat Sound System's rankin' selector. He then moved into engineering and production at Studio One, starting his own production company when he tired of toiling long hours for Coxsone's alleged low pay. The Wailers was one of the first acts he produced and Perry, unlike Kong and Dodd, remained friends with Marley, despite some serious spats.

The Wailers stopped working with Dodd shortly after 'Bus' Dem Shut' was released. "The man rob we," said Bob, a common refrain of artists of that time who sold their art for small sums simply to survive. But, as Chris Blackwell points out, it was their choice. "The way it was done then is that everyone wanted a flat fee (regretting it when they found out that there was money to be made on the back end). There was no real industry... and when there is no royalty system in place, it always makes sense to sell something outright." He goes on to note that the producers were "not really taking advantage of the artists, it was the only logical way of dealing with it."

What Blackwell denounces is the practice by some Jamaican producers of not compensating these artists properly when old tracks got new life and royalties were reaped on the rebounds. During another interview Blackwell says that because royalties were not being paid to The Wailers on any of their early material, he had suggested to them that they re-cut many of the songs recorded for those first producers and reclaim the publishing and other rights that had been taken away from them.

Royalty issues aside, however, The Wailers worked well with Scratch Perry (and dealt well with idiosyncrasies like Perry's preference for recording in mono because he believed in the "unity of one" and that stereo had a split personality).

On songs like 'Duppy Conqueror', 'Soul Almighty', 'Try Me', 'Cornerstone', 'Kaya' and 'Small Axe', Perry not only pared away the excess from The Wailers' sound, he also created a tension and mood in the group's music that Marley carried forward into his later work.

Perry's production of The Wailers coincided with the birth of reggae – what Bob Marley called "earth feelin' music". The short era of rock-steady, which ruled after ska, was already giving way to the hypnotic "riddim" that would take Jamaican music to every place on the planet, the music's addictive power and worldwide appeal due in part to Marley himself, but also a reflection of the creative energy surging out of Kingston during those early times. Sly Dunbar describes this period as "wicked – there was live music everywhere and the studios were full all the time".

Perry not only gave The Wailers a more distinct sound, he also gave them – albeit unwittingly – the musicians who would become first a part

"WE WERE SO MUCH IN LOVE WITH THE MUSIC AND WITH WHAT WE WERE DOING THAT MONEY COULD NOT COME BETWEEN US AND THAT MUSIC."
BUNNY WAILER

of the original Wailers, and then a couple of years down the road Marley's backing band. Drum and bass brothers, Carlton (Carly) and Aston (Family Man) Barrett, who were the rhythm section of Perry's house band, The Upsetters, would, along with Bob on rhythm guitar, Peter on keys and lead guitar, and Bunny on percussion, become the new Wailers band in good time for the first Island album, *Catch A Fire*.

Marley never saw himself as much of a musician, but said that when session players, tired of being ripped off by producers, began making themselves unavailable for sessions, The Wailers had no choice but to "start playin' ourselves". Bassist, Family Man Barrett, who met Bob at The Wailers' second retail record shop on Orange Street –"where he used to sit outside and reason, sometimes for the whole day" – taught Marley most of what he knew about guitar. "He used to say that he could have been a better guitar player, but 'Family Man won't teach me any more chords'."

To call the mid- to late-Sixties the golden age of Jamaican music is an understatement. On every street corner sat a songwriter. And at every studio gate stood a long line of hopefuls, each with a surefire hit song for any producer who would bite. If the singer impressed the producer enough to get called into the studio, the routine was simple and swift. "We would

PRODUCER JOE GIBBS'
RECORD SHOP ON
NEW KINGSTON.

25

line up and sing a tune a cappella," says Junior Tucker, who began singing professionally at the age of five, "so that the keyboard player could get the chords." The bass player would then find a line, and the drummer catch a groove and the rhythm track was laid. The vocalist had a maximum of two takes to lay down a decent vocal. "Every man haffi come sharp," is how Tucker puts it, noting that for those who couldn't make it, there was always a "ringmaster" like Robbie Shakespeare ready to show them to the door. "Robbie would lick their back with his bass if they didn't move out fast enough," Tucker laughs. As he tells it, "half of the equipment didn't work, and at Channel One there was even a hole in the wall, but they'd just plug up the hole or push in a bit of paper to hold a loose plug, and go again."

Somehow out of this chaos came perfection. And the musicians knew it. It was the reason Bob Marley would later "allow the madness at 56 Hope Road", say several of those who were part of it, and the reason people like Sly and Robbie continue to record at sessions jam-packed with people "hanging in" or "passing through". Says Sly: "It's the vibes."

"Harry J's studio was known for the vibes," says Cat Coore, lead guitar player for the band, Third World, who were recording at Harry J's at the same time as The Wailers. "It wasn't the best in terms of equipment," says Coore. "It had its little quirks, but Harry J is a good man and everyone liked recording there"

BUNNY WAILER: "THE WAILERS' DESIGN WAS ALWAYS TO IMPROVE."

The Wailers had moved to Harry Johnson's Roosevelt Avenue studio as they got better at their craft, feeling – despite disagreement from various producers and other musicians who remained loyal to the earlier studios – that they were getting a better sound there than what they could get at any of the earlier, downtown rooms.

Unlike those first studios, Harry J's was uptown, just a short drive away from the town's two main hotels, the Jamaica Pegasus, and the then Kingston Sheraton (which until 1984 was the only place in Jamaica with an escalator). "When Harry is opened for us ghetto people," says Tucker, "it was a revelation. It was Jamaica's first well-run studio." Harry J's was also the first studio which had been set up more for recording albums than singles. Harry J's clients were more likely to block book time, than to come for a little three-hour session.

As for Harry J himself, who has always felt that his contribution to Jamaica's music and to the production of The Wailers has never been fully recognized, he was a man who had enough vision to realise that reggae could reach the rest of the world, and to produce music that although considered "soft" at the time by the hardcore set, continued – like The Wailers' music – to bridge the gap between local reggae and international pop. 'Bed's Too Big' by Sheila Hylton is a good example of his work – and one which was mocked by Jamaican purists incensed that a Jamaican producer had done a cover of a "white reggae" tune… until the song was a big hit in England. The consensus now is that Harry J was a remarkable producer with a good sense of sound whose role in the development of Jamaican music and the success of The Wailers was vastly underrated.

Marley's studio habits had been formed very early on. A stickler for punctuality – "He was always the first one on the tour bus," says Chris Blackwell – and military-like precision, he was a man on a God-given mission who had no time to waste, especially studio time that he was paying for. His music and his message were his life, and taken more seriously than anything else – women included.

But Bunny, Peter and Bob were still a trio at this point in The Wailers' career, and both shared Marley's commitment to solid production. Bunny Wailer sums up that magical time: "We were so much in love with the music and with what we were doing that money could not come between us and that music. Money couldn't get near. That's why these guys were always creaming and ripping us off, because The Wailers weren't worried about money. We were trying to build our artistry so that when we heard what we'd done we'd be satisfied." But The Wailers didn't stay satisfied for long.

"THERE WAS LIVE MUSIC EVERYWHERE AND THE STUDIOS WERE FULL ALL THE TIME."

SLY DUNBAR

"The Wailers' design was always to improve… every member of The Wailers was like that. You could hear it in the work."

Yet neither were The Wailers completely devoid of business ambition. In 1966, they established Wail'n Soul'm imprint. In 1969, Tuff Gong Export was taken as a trade name to distinguish the records that were being sent abroad. In 1970, they opened a Tuff Gong shop on Orange Street, which then moved to 127 King Street and, in 1973, the name was formalized via incorporation, first as Tough Gang Records, and then changed a month later to Tuff Gong Records Limited. Each of The Wailers received 1,331 shares. Tuff Gong – a symbol of what once was – would continue to be The Wailers' label for some time after the musical alliance broke up, but then fell dormant until it was reactivated in 1983 by Bunny Wailer. He ran a full-page advert in Jamaica's *Daily Gleaner* in 1996, denouncing the fact that Chris Blackwell had quietly attempted to appropriate the name in 1990 (and apparently succeeded).

BUS' DEM SHUT (PYAKA)

Produced by The Wailers at Dynamics in 1966, and released on their Wail'n Soul'm label as The Wailing Wailers – the short-lived variant on their original name – this recording pretty well sums up what they were beginning to feel from certain quarters of society. A "pyaka" is an envious person and "to cut down pyakaism" is a plea to let go of the envy and work together, a plea still being aired daily in this land where covetousness is said to be the national malaise. Jealousy is prevalent everywhere, but in Jamaica it is especially vicious. Were it not for this dark side to the national psyche, some believe that many of Jamaica's ills would be resolved.

"Jamaica is a place," said Bob, "where you really build up competition in your mind. People here feel they must fight against me and I must fight against you… Jealousy. Suspicion. Anger. Poverty. Competition. We should just get together and create music."

SCREWFACE

Bob Marley was known, like his father, to be a serious "screwface" (someone with an angry or mean expression). He also possessed a nasty temper which exploded whenever anyone (especially one of his women) tested his patience. Intimates knew when to steer clear of him and not test The Skipper. But the screwface spoken of in the song is not Bob – it's the

13, which includes Trench Town, is considered the worst of addresses, and no one had ever "bigged the residents up" in song before Bob.

The subtle and socially constructive suggestion in the lyric that music can protect and empower "You can't come cold I up" (kill me) better than the gun, because when music hits "you feel no pain", is in marked contrast to the stark negativity of 1999's "anytime mi hungry agin, dem a guh si mi nine (millimetre gun)". That line, taken from DJ Bounty Killa's controversial Number One song 'Anytime', sums up the dramatic shift in Jamaica's music since the halcyon days of The Skipper.

HIGH TIDE OR LOW TIDE

THE YOUNG MARLEY COUPLE WITH FAMILY. (LEFT TO RIGHT, SHARON, ZIGGY, CEDELLA, AND IN CARRIAGE, STEVEN.)

This song was recorded in 1969. Produced by The Wailers and briefly considered for the *Catch A Fire* album, it was mixed in 1972. But 'High Tide Or Low Tide' was not released until Island Records' *Songs Of Freedom* appeared in 1992. Musically, the track misses, and is not up to the level of other Wailers work. The melody is unremarkable, the harmony is loose, and the arrangement reminiscent of second-rate R&B.

33

It's not hard to understand why it was collectively decided to hold it back until 1992 when there was little else remaining that hadn't already been heard. But 'High Tide Or Low Tide' does have a memorable lyric and had the makings of a beautiful song if a bit more time been spent on finding a melody that did it justice and running just one more take on the vocals.

By all accounts, Bob Marley loved children and tried, despite his peripatetic lifestyle, to be a good father to all his offspring – legitimately begotten or otherwise – and to give them the protection he cites his mother as asking for in this song. Themes that allow for dual interpretation are a constant in Marley's writing and 'High Tide Or Low Tide' is a good example. The chorus is about being a good friend in both high and low seas, which could be applied to anyone. The verses, however, pin it down to his being there for his children.

CATCH A FIRE

1972

PRODUCED BY: CHRIS BLACKWELL AND BOB MARLEY

STIR IT UP

SLAVE DRIVER

MIDNIGHT RAVERS

CONCRETE JUNGLE

BABY WE'VE GOT A DATE (ROCK IT BABY)

NO MORE TROUBLE

KINKY REGGAE

The most critical connexion in Marley's career was made in London, 1972, when The Wailers went to see Chris Blackwell, head of the independent Island Records, then one of the hottest labels in rock.

Only a barefoot island boy with good breeding – a streetwise sophisticate – could have created Island Records. Such a boy was Christopher Blackwell.

Born in London just before World War II, Blackwell was carried home to Jamaica, by boat, at the age of six months, by his Irish father, Joseph, and Jewish-Jamaican mother, Blanche. "Christopher has never forgiven me for having been born in England instead of in Jamaica," says Blanche Blackwell.

At the age of 10, like all Jamaican children of his colour and class, Christopher Blackwell returned to England to attend boarding school, in his case, Harrow, which he attended for several years. A rebel and an entrepreneur even then, the 17-year-old schoolboy – after a humbling public caning – was expelled for selling liquor and cigarettes to fellow pupils.

Back in Jamaica, Chris Blackwell hung out with well-connected friends of his parents, such as Errol Flynn (who had a house in Port Antonio), and Ian Fleming (whose *GoldenEye* property in Oracabessa, Blackwell would one day buy), and got his first taste of the entertainment business as a location scout for the James Bond film, *Dr No*.

Much to his mother's distress – "I wanted Christopher to be a chartered accountant and sent him to Price Waterhouse" – Blackwell then started dabbling in music, finding a ready market in Jamaica for rare R&B 78s picked up in New York and re-sold, without an identifying label, for a decent profit.

CHRIS BLACKWELL, ONE OF THE MOST SIGNIFICANT PLAYERS IN THE BOB MARLEY STORY.

Next, he went into music production for himself but finding, despite three local hits in a row, that doing business in the cut-throat Kingston market had major limitations, he decided to move back to Britain, and, instead of competing with his rivals, distribute their music overseas, which he did through a one-half interest in a company called Trojan Records.

Island Records, named from the famous Alec Waugh novel, *Island In The Sun*, was founded in 1962, the same year that the Union Jack was lowered for the last time, and the new Jamaican flag of black, green and gold (symbolizing hardship, fertility and sunshine, respectively) rose to the ecstatic cheers of a country that believed itself to be on the brink of a brilliant future. It was an exciting, if turbulent, time in the Caribbean and Blackwell fed off the raw energy that flowed from this changing order. Crossing social and colour lines to understand, and absorb, the power of a music that had suddenly sprung from a people finally free from colonial restraint, Blackwell took a modest investment of £5,000 (which 30 years later would give him a $350 million return) and started his label.

His first hit, Millie Small's six-million-seller, 'My Boy Lollipop', came quickly. Flush with this beginner's luck, Blackwell signed a slew of British rock acts and temporarily took his attention away from the music that had got him started. Jimmy Cliff and Perry Henzell's classic film of the ghetto, *The Harder They Come*, got him back in.

For a short while, Jimmy Cliff was Island's main focus. "I was so excited about where we could go with him," says Blackwell, remembering how upset he was when he and Cliff fell out and the singer signed with EMI. But as Jimmy Cliff walked out of Island's door, Bob Marley and The Wailers walked in. "Off the street," says Blackwell.

Through his interest in Trojan Records, Blackwell had already released a few Wailers singles, including 'Simmer Down', which, at the time, he recalls, "was just another record". He even spelled Marley's name wrong. But when he met them in person he sensed that the trio had something he could work with, noting that Bob bore a striking character resemblance to Rhygin', the real-life gangster that Jimmy Cliff's role in the Henzell film was based upon. "He was a combination of rebel, gangster and street poet," he said in one interview, "and I thought he could be as big as Jimi Hendrix."

In 1972, The Wailers were in England with Danny Sims who had enticed them there with a basic deal with CBS and the plan that they were to tour as the opening act for Johnny Nash (then in the UK charts with his reggae-flavoured hit, 'I Can See Clearly Now'). When the tour didn't pan out, and CBS failed to promote the single, 'Reggae On Broadway',

"SLAVE DRIVER THE TABLE IS TURNED, CATCH A FIRE SO YOU CAN GET BURNED."
BOB MARLEY

JIMMY CLIFF POSES
IN FRONT OF A
POSTER FOR *THE
HARDER THEY COME*
– THE FILM THAT
LAUNCHED
HIS CAREER.

one of the trio had the idea of checking their countryman, Chris Blackwell, at Island's Notting Hill headquarters. A mutual Jamaican connexion set up a meeting.

Chris Blackwell had already been warned that The Wailers were "trouble" – Bunny Wailer remembers Blackwell telling them he'd heard they were "killers and cannibals", adding, he was very surprised that we were civilised people." Some questioned Blackwell's decision to give the group £4,000 (in those days a hefty sum for Jamaican musicians) to take back home to record an album, but he was a gambler both by inheritance and inclination, and he believed that this small advance (sweetened with the promise of a further £4,000 on delivery), not to mention his decision to pay a similar sum, with an override on the next six albums, to buy out the CBS contract, would pay off.

Not surprisingly to those who know just how good a gambler he is, Blackwell's bet on the three Trench Town boys (who he had advised to drop their dated vocal trio concept in favour of a "tight, live band") proved sound. By the end of the year, when the head of Island went back to Jamaica for a visit, he was picked up at his New Kingston hotel by the band, driven to the studio for a listening session, and got to carry back to England, in his words, "one of the best albums ever put out."

Catch A Fire, the first concept album in reggae's short and single-driven history, was recorded by the three Wailers in Kingston at Harry J's, Randy's and Dynamic (where the following year the Stones would go to record *Goat's Head Soup*). Still lacking the ability to play their own instruments, the threesome were aided by two of the musicians who would themselves one day become Wailers – Aston "Family Man" Barrett on bass, and his brother, Carlton (Carly) on drums. Family Man doesn't remember exactly how much studio time cost in those days, but the album was likely recorded for a steal. Jamaican musicians learned early on to work hard and fast, sometimes cutting several songs in one day.

Robbie Shakespeare, bassist of drum and bass duo Sly & Robbie, speaks affectionately of the days almost 30 years ago when, as a young

teenager, he played bass for Bob Marley And The Wailers, on a session that produced two of their best songs: 'Concrete Jungle' and 'Stir It Up'. "Playing on a session in that time come like nuttin'," he says. "But playing on a Wailers session was something." He remembers that on this particular session, "there was great discussion about the intro to 'Concrete Jungle', then when I found a line for the song, Bunny gave me a little part at the front and it all come together" Less time was spent on 'Stir It Up', a simpler song and, for the experienced Kingston session men who played, it was an easy couple of hours' work. "In those days," says

, "they would run down (rehearse) a song a long time before putting it on tape." Studio time was, for these ghetto musicians, a valuable commodity, not a minute of which could be wasted.

When it came to paying the musicians, things were also tight. Even when (as in The Wailers' case) an advance on production was paid, the way it was (and still is) done in Jamaica was that the more the budget could be squeezed, the more would be left over for the group. Laughing as he tells the story, Shakespeare says that his session fee per song was then JA$10–$15 (around £20-£30 at the time) "but at the end of that day, we nevah get paid."

About a week after leaving The Wailers at Harry J's, Shakespeare went to check Marley at his downtown record shop. "They had a sign outside – it was either Tuff Gong or Intel Diplo (Tosh's label), or maybe it was both – and Bob was leaning on a headpost beside it. We reasoned a while and when it was time to move out, it come money time. Bob gave me some money, but I only got paid for one song – $15.00." But there were no hard feelings. Back in the first bloom of Jamaican pop music, recalls Shakespeare, "it was the norm that if you were doing five songs, the producer would say, 'I can pay for three, beg you for one and owe you for one.' It was like a tight-knit family."

At this point in the conversation, Shakespeare stops in amazement. Throughout the interview, a radio tuned to Power 102, a station not known to present much Marley fare, has been playing in the background. Then, the opening notes of *Catch A Fire*, the intro that Shakespeare has just been talking about are heard. "Rahtid," says Robbie. "See Bob deh." It is one of those intense, goose-pimple moments. Even a rude bwoy like Robbie Shakespeare is a little shaken. "I've got chills all down my back." It was February, 1999, in Kingston, but for a second it was 1972 and *Catch A Fire* was still in production.

"PLAYING ON A SESSION IN THAT TIME COME LIKE NUTTIN', BUT PLAYING ON A WAILERS SESSION WAS SOMETHING."
ROBBIE SHAKESPEARE

In the Island Basing Street basement studio known as the Fallout Shelter, the basic tracks were, as Blackwell says, "incredible", but the Island head's additional production gave the album an international pop passport, via overdubs of sounds familiar to rock ears, the guitar licks of Alabama's Wayne Perkins being the most effective. They called Perkins the "white Wailer" and today the man who gave 'Concrete Jungle' what Robbie Shakespeare calls "that wicked, wicked solo", ruefully reveals that he never really got credit for his contribution. He is also disappointed that repeated requests for a gold record have been ignored.

Perkins had been working on a second Smith, Perkins and Smith album for Island when "Chris stopped me on the spiral staircase going up to the top studio – the main room. He said there was a Wailer project he wanted me to play on. I said, 'Who are The Wailers?' Chris said, 'They play reggae' and I said, 'That don't help me." After a brief rundown on reggae, Blackwell told Perkins, "Just get your Fender, your Les Paul and an amp, and come on down." Says Perkins, "I was a 20-year-old boy from Alabama confronted by these wild-looking Rastas from Jamaica. I had no idea what I was getting into."

It was the first time Perkins had heard reggae – "Desmond Dekker wasn't reggae to me, it was too much R&B – and I said, 'Where is my

"A SONG WITH AN URGENT, CONTEMPORARY EDGE… COMPLEX AND BRILLIANT."
CHRIS BLACKWELL

bass on 'Concrete Jungle', which quickly caught on as yet another of The Wailers' anthems.

On the flip side of the 'Concrete Jungle' single put out by Island Records was a song called 'Reincarnated Souls', which, according to Bunny Wailer, had originally been pegged to be the title track of their sophomore album. This album was retitled *Burnin'* after Bunny Wailer "made his stance" against Island plans that clashed with his principles.

'Concrete Jungle' is described by Chris Blackwell as "complex, brilliant". It is a track that nearly 40 years later has still retained its contemporary and urgent edge.

ROCK IT BABY

'Rock It Baby' is a classic Bob Marley uptempo love song. Written in the ska style of the day, the banal lyrics (yes, he was capable of banality) are compensated for by the seductive and rollicking role of a ska shuffle stretched in a reggae direction by a "cheng cheng" rhythm guitar. The Wayne Perkins addition of a Santa and Johnny-ish steel guitar – "It was a slide guitar with open G tuning," Perkins notes – stretches the track even further from its Kingston roots without breaking the connection. "I wanted to make it different," says Perkins. "I listened to the harmony and the spacing in between for where I could come in." Elaborating further, Perkins says that he "always listens for the counter melody, I either go with it or against it, and if you listen to it you can hear the different changes going by… about six or seven chords in transition. I worked on it for a while, adding a note here and there. With open G tuning you can do anything… mostly by playing harmony thirds" The end result Perkins describes as "almost Hawaiian Island-ish."

Throughout his career, Marley the militant soldier was criticised for his lyrics of lighter mood. Hard yard artistes are supposed to keep their sex and love lives to themselves. The irony in Marley's case is that he started off singing mostly love songs. The really serious stuff came later. Danny Sims, in particular, resisted all Rasta content in his productions, and said that he wanted to break Bob in the States by blending his lovers rock reggae with R&B.

Chris Blackwell, a renegade himself, was the first not only to encourage, but to embrace the singer's rebel side, giving Marley (who believed that truth was synonymous with Rastafari) and the other Wailers free rein to record what they wanted.

45

NO MORE TROUBLE

Trouble walks everywhere in Jamaica, especially in ghetto enclaves like TrenchTown. Contradicting this tradition, The Wailers' message was one of peace and "livity" instead of war and destruction... and when they spoke, the ghetto was starting to listen. "What is there to benefit from badness?" asked Marley, who preached that unity was the future and that tribal violence belonged in the past.

No More Trouble' gets its positive point across with little more than a short, powerful plea and a great hook. That Peter Tosh, a man who courted trouble, arranged it is obvious from the first couple of notes – the interplay of instruments around a trademark Tosh bass line creates a sort of street drama that is often heard in his later work. Marley's soulful vocal

THE POLITICAL AFFILIATION OF THIS AREA OF TRENCH TOWN IS CLARIFIED BY THE PNP SIGN.

THE ROLLING STONES
TOOK THE TITLE OF
THEIR HIT 'BROWN
SUGAR' FROM THE
JAMAICAN SLANG FOR
A SEXY BROWN GIRL.

injects a soft twist that balances the tension implied by the music, and, as he once avowed was his mission, he "overcomes the Devil with a thing called love".

The ability to straddle opposites is a key element in explaining Marley's impact. Unlike Peter Tosh – an equally talented but less influential figure – Bob Marley saw many sides, and once told an interviewer that 'man mus' stan' up fi 'im right, an' nah give up 'im right, but me nah gwin fight fi me right" (a belief only tested when he spoke of Africa). Tosh, on the other hand, had no such qualms.

KINKY REGGAE

Tales of The Skipper's "dark" side are freely told "off the record" by some intimates. By rock standards, these kinky indulgences were mild, and, predictably, mostly related to women (with whom he exhibited strong symptoms of a love-hate complex that at times led to violence).

The promised intrigue of the lyrics of 'Kinky Reggae' "brown sugar" was a popular slang term favoured by the original R&B artists (later famously appropriated by The Rolling Stones) meaning sexy brown girl, and "booga wooga" – which can be figured out – are not matched by the music itself, which suffers from a fairly pedantic arrangement, and which has no innovative add-ons by outside musicians to liven it up.

BURNIN'

Some of the tracks on *Burnin'* had been recorded at the same time as *Catch A Fire*, but the album was completed at Harry J's Studio in the middle of 1973. Harry J's, on Kingston's Roosevelt Avenue, is now deserted; its doors locked, and its yard silent. But signs of its illustrious past still linger. A beautifully evocative, eye-level portrait of Bob on the cream courtyard wall bears quiet witness to the scene that was and is no longer. Other portraits of artists that featured in Harry J's past also remain behind, as does a large and colourful painting of a guitar on the trunk of a shady mango tree.

Standing alone in the waning light of a sultry February afternoon, there is an eerie, but not uncomfortable, sense of The Wailers' presence – the echo of the mystical music they made at Harry J's still hanging heavily in the otherwise silent air.

In the beginning, production and arrangement tasks were fairly evenly shared between the three Wailers, but, gradually, Marley took on the responsibility of finishing tracks, as it became clear that the group was not going to survive in its three-man, three-vote format.

Chris Blackwell was in on the mix, just as he had been for *Catch A Fire* – "doubling the length of the songs, overdubbing, stretching them out like rock songs, and adding instrumental breaks".

On hearing this, manager Don Taylor is adamant that Blackwell brought little to the production end, but others, like engineer Errol Thomson, who was on the board for many of The Wailers' recording and mixing sessions, acknowledge his considerable contribution: "He knows when to bring in this and take out that."

Blackwell is not surprised by Taylor's assertion, but is equally adamant in defending his creative input. Much of the dispute about Blackwell's right to be credited in this way is likely to stem from the confusion within Jamaica's music industry on what exactly a producer's role is. The common understanding within the trade is that only musicians or engineers produce. The public at large think the "producer" is the executive producer – "the man with the money". The creative producer with an ear is not understood, and that's what Blackwell is. "I think I've got an ear for music, a feel for what good music is." Sly and Robbie go one further: "Chris is a musical prophet."

As to what it was like working with The Wailers in the studio, Blackwell, interviewed in 1999, makes mention of how long ago it was – "27 years" – and then says that he worked with all three only once, "for a very short period in England. It was on *Burnin'*... it was very short, maybe one tune, or two tunes, something like that... I think they were on tour, because they came up to us (from another part of England) for a short time and left."

The tour was for *Catch A Fire* – first the UK and then the United States. But, before the US leg started, Bunny Wailer dropped out and Joe Higgs, The Wailers' first mentor, filled in.

Bunny would rejoin the group for an aborted opening slot for the US tour of Sly & The Family Stone (after four shows they were bumped, reportedly for being better than the headliners), as well as the start of the *Burnin'* tour in the UK. This tour, too, was aborted after a show in the British Midlands town of Northampton where, according to tour manager Mick Cater, a flu-stricken Tosh took the onset of thick snow as a sign that "the tour was doomed", which it then became when The Wailers cancelled all remaining dates and boarded a hastily-booked Air Jamaica flight back to Kingston.

The commonly accepted reason behind Bunny's departure from the group is that he didn't want to fly – and it is true that he has a phobia about travelling on the "iron bird". But, Bunny tells a different version. "I left because of spiritual reasons... the plans that were made for The Wailers and the direction that The Wailers would be going, I didn't as a Rastaman think I should be going in that direction, so I made a stand on behalf of my other brothers with the intent that they would back me up." But they didn't, and Bunny Wailer decided to back out. "I was just one monkey who don't spoil no show," he muses, sadly.

Sitting outside Mixing Lab Studio on the kind of muggy Kingston morning that can make a New York summer seem cool, the last living Wailer (Peter Tosh was murdered in 1987) is outspoken about his decision to leave The Wailers just when things were getting interesting.

"I LEFT THE WAILERS BECAUSE OF SPIRITUAL REASONS."
BUNNY WAILER

BUNNY WAILER,
THE ONLY SURVIVING
MEMBER OF THE
ORIGINAL WAILERS.

"Chris wanted to put us in nightclubs… "freak" clubs. When I asked him why, he said, 'The Wailers are nobody, so we have to play in these places to be somebody.' I said, 'I'm not gonna be anybody… bodies are buried… so I just ease off the body plan."

With Bunny gone, it didn't take long for a rift to develop between the strong-willed Peter Tosh and the equally forceful Blackwell (who Tosh liked to call "Whitewell"). "Peter was very difficult," says Blackwell. "Bunny could be, too, but at least if he wasn't going to do something, he'd say so. With Peter, he'd say 'yes', and then not do it,"

Marley was more charitable, saying of his old friend Tosh's contrariness that "he wanted to have the adventures himself. Him talented enough an' maybe him waan somethin' better dan dis."

Burnin' – the last album the original three Wailers would record together – would also be the last time the Island head and Tosh would work together. The final break came when Blackwell refused to put out Tosh's solo album because it would have interfered with the marketing plan he had for Marley.

Blackwell's and Bunny Wailer's relationship lasted longer, but the three friends from Trench Town who formed a musical group and called themselves The Wailers were together no longer, and Bob Marley was now Island's sole focus.

Family Man Barrett picks up the story: "Bob said to me, 'What are we going to do now, there's only the three of us left?' So I said, 'Well, the three of us (Bob, Family Man and brother Carly) will just go back on the road." Continuing with the air of a man who remembers something as clearly as if it was yesterday, Family Man puts the event into context. "Now, this was also the time that we were supposed to start recording again, and trus' me, *Natty Dread* (as the third Island album would be titled) started off as a dreadful situation. But then Bob said he'd book the time at Harry J's, call in Glaston Anderson on keyboards, Winston Wright on organ, and a couple of horn players, and we just moved on."

In 1975, Marley reminisced about the split, attributing it to a growing difference in priorities. "Is like dem (Bunny and Peter) don't waan understand dat me cyaan jus' play music for Jamaica alone. Cyaan learn dat way. Me get de mos' learnin' when me travel and talk to other people." He also mentioned that learning was not the only reason he needed to leave the island. "Me aff leave certain times because of politics and politicians wanting favours. Dem love come to you and try get you, and me is a man dat nuh like turn down no man. So me leave Jamaica."

Not surprisingly, his two former bandmates saw things in a slightly different way. Although Bunny Wailer refused to blame Chris Blackwell for the break-up, he noted nonetheless that the label boss had wanted to allow for this possibility right from the beginning: "I saw it in a contract... the first (Island) contract... it stated that The Wailers could be split into different areas and sent as individuals to perform... and that was never the intention of The Wailers."

Pausing for effect, his eyes burning with a tinge of lingering anger, Wailer describes how the group tore up that initial contract, and says, "It was presumptuous, telling us in our face that the plans were to split (us)." But, having said this, Bunny Wailer is realistic, and understands that no one could have come between "bredren" who were solidly together, and if all had been well. "In the end, it was up to us," he concludes philosophically. "It was our choice."

"ONCE MONEY STARTED TO BE MADE AND PEOPL GOT FAMOUS, EVERYTHING CHANGED."
PETER TOSH

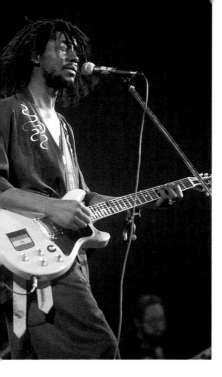

Peter Tosh never reached the point of reason where he was able to see it like Bunny Wailer. In a conversation at his house in Kingston, in the same room where just a few days later he would be brutally murdered by six gunmen, Tosh, sitting in a high-backed wicker chair, smoking a Peter Tosh-sized spliff (rolled from a large, plastic bag of ganja that sat at his feet), spoke bitterly about The Wailers' break-up and the years thereafter. "Bob Marley was my student," he said simply, before summing up what happened: "Once money started to be made and people got famous, everything changed."

Many years after The Wailers went their separate ways, Tosh would be accused of gouging the eyes out of a portrait of his one-time friend and musical partner that hung in the studio at Music Mountain, Jamaica's best recording facility in the Eighties. After he'd cut out the eyes with a penknife, Tosh supposedly turned the painting

53

A YOUNG PETER TOSH: DESPITE HIS MILITANT IMAGE AND "DIFFICULT" REPUTATION HE WAS KNOWN AMONG HIS FRIENDS FOR HIS KINDNESS.

around so that it would be facing the wall rather than himself, who refused to record with a dead man watching him. Tosh, however, staunchly denied any involvement in this bizarre incident.

As a final note on the dissolution of one of the most gifted trios in the history of pop music, Bunny Wailer was keen to stress the positive, while acknowledging that problems still continue. "With The Wailers solo, you get double, triple, The Wailers' work… it benefited the music, it benefited us as individuals, because we didn't make any money until we split. All the work that we did together as The Wailers, that's still left hanging there, nobody has collected those monies. All the work that we did with Coxsone, Lee Perry, Beverley's, all those monies were pirated, and we've never got anything out of that."

"Nesta", according to Marley's mother, means "messenger". Appropriately enough, *Burnin'* made an enormous word-of-mouth impact on both sides of the Atlantic on its release in 1974. Still relatively unknown in the mainstream music market at the time, The Wailers had acquired an enviable underground reputation which critical praise of *Burnin'* solidified.

The album artwork – photographs once again by Chris Blackwell's girlfriend, Esther Anderson – maintained the ghetto feel of *Catch A Fire*, with a black-and-white relief image of the group against a brown board background on the front of the sleeve. Inside is another relief image, this one of Marley smoking a replica of the spliff he sported on the cover of *Catch A Fire*.

Three of the songs on *Burnin'* were not written by Marley. 'One Foundation' was Tosh-penned and performed, and both 'Hallelujah' and 'Pass It On' (stylistically out-of-character tunes for The Wailers) were the work of a now probably wealthy "Jean Watt".

Track for track, *Burnin'* is as good a collection, but not better than *Catch A Fire*. Outstanding cuts like 'Get Up Stand Up', the LP's opening track, and 'I Shot the Sheriff', compare with the previous album's 'Concrete Jungle' and No More Trouble'.

In retrospect, however, both releases seem to hover between the sound of The Wailers as they had been, and as they would have become had they not self-destructed.

BURNIN, AND LOOTIN'

"Dat song about burnin' and lootin' is (about) illusions… the illusions of capitalists and dem people with the big bank accounts," said Marley.

To say that 'Burnin' And Lootin'' was controversial in a country where angry, frustrated people routinely block roads with burning tyres just to have their voices heard, is far too mild a way to describe the song's actual impact. Jamaica's volatile society has always been very open to the incendiary messages of its musical idols. Although Marley could say a couple of years later that the tune was about "illusions", what it was really about was "burnin' and lootin'" and giving the ghetto youth the go-ahead to help themselves.

Curfews are no longer as common in Jamaica as they once were in the Seventies, and when they're enforced they're usually in some way warranted. But as well as being useful in curbing spontaneous outbreaks of violence, curfews are also a clever way to control rebellion. With the growing influence of Rasta and reggae music, rebellion of the self-styled "sufferahs" was but a drum beat away, and the authorities had to find a way to stop it.

"Babylon nuh waan peace, Babylon waan power," was Bob's defence of his militant approach. "My songs have a message of righteousness," he explained. But in another interview, he made it clear that he wasn't a pacifist. "Me don' love fighting, but me don' love wickedness either"

GET UP STAND UP

Used as a unifying anthem by Amnesty International in the era of its big-name candlelight concerts for the cause of human rights, from a political perspective this is Bob Marley's most powerful song. Although the words are more suited to the no-bullshit baritone of Peter Tosh, Bob's soulful wail takes the edge off Peter's stridency and the duet works better than either of their later solo efforts.

In 1975, Marley said of this song, "It say man can live." But by 1978, he was frustrated by its failure to immediately change things. "How long must I protest the same things? I sing 'Get Up Stand Up', and up till now people don't get up." If alive today, he would be desperately frustrated. In 21st-century Jamaica people still haven't stood up to an increasingly oppressive and corrupt system. "But dat don' mean dem won'," says Far I, a Trench Town street dread who grew up with Bob. "It jus' tek time."

Ironically, this song, which was one of the last that Peter and Bob would record together, was, says Junior Tucker who heard the story from Rita Marley, also the catalyst for their one post-split reunion – at a club in London. Bob Marley and the second set of Wailers were appearing live. As Marley began a standard delivery of 'Get Up Stand Up', the audience responded vocally as they always did and, by the second verse, they were on their feet. When the band came out of the second chorus ready to hit the third verse, the lead voice suddenly changed as Peter Tosh, microphone in hand, strode on to the stage, shocking Bob as much as the audience. As Tosh's powerful baritone began singing, "We're sick and tired of your isms and schism game," it brought the house down, and a beaming Bob let Peter have the spotlight, skanking beside him in undisguised joy.

At the song's end, Peter turned to a nodding Bob and said, "The Queen feel dat one deh." Then, handing the microphone back to his former bandmate, he left as quickly as he had come. They never spoke again.

"THE ELEMENTS OF THAT SONG IS PEOPLE BEEN JUDGING YOU AND YOU CAN'T STAND IT NO MORE AND YOU EXPLODE, YOU JUST EXPLODE."
BOB MARLEY

55

I SHOT THE SHERIFF

Eric Clapton came across Bob Marley's music quite by accident. As he tells it, he was in the middle of making his critically and commercially successful album, *461 Ocean Boulevard*, at Miami's Criteria Studio when guitarist George Terry played him the *Burnin'* album.

Clapton's cover of 'I Shot The Sheriff' was an immediate worldwide hit. Not only did it revitalize Clapton's solo career, but it exposed the work of Bob Marley to a much wider audience. The song's wicked combination of "Wild West" lyrical hook and killer guitar riff cemented it solidly in the minds of the millions who tuned into pop radio in the summer of 1974.

Reflecting on the writing of the song, Marley said, "I wanted to say, 'I shot the police', but because the (Jamaican) government would have made a fuss, I changed it to 'I shot the sheriff' instead." Changing the intended target didn't change the meaning, though: "It's the same idea, justice." And the inspiration for the song: "The elements of that song is people been judging you and you can't stand it no more and you explode, you just explode."

Clapton, unfamiliar with Caribbean ways, asked Marley, after it was recorded, to explain the song. "Him like the kind of music, and him like the melody (but) he didn't know the meaning of the words" Even without the complete understanding he sought, however, Clapton instinctively caught the beat, and came up with a faultless version of what would rival 'Tears In Heaven' as some of his best-known work.

ERIC CLAPTON: "IT TOOK ME A WHILE TO GET INTO IT TO TELL YOU THE TRUTH," HE SAID OF 'I SHOT THE SHERIFF'.

As for whether the original singer resented that someone else made his song a hit, Bob Marley was more than gracious: "We do our own version, but it couldn't be a hit single because the quality wasn't there at the time, and if someone do over a song, maybe they can make it a bit better than the first person who do it."

PUT IT ON

A new version of the ska song that marked the marriage celebration of Robert and Rita Marley, this updated rocksteady rendition, like the other old Wailer titles that the group re-did for Island Records, reflected not only the progress in The Wailers' musical ability, but also the additional input of Chris Blackwell after the eight-track tapes had been delivered to Island Records.

Blackwell was also the person behind the idea of re-cutting The Wailers' previous work. "Early on, Bob had problems collecting from these

"WI LICKLE BUT WI TALLEWAH" JAMAICAN PHRASE MEANING "SMALL BUT STRONG".

first records because three different people claimed… it's something that's still going on to this day. I'd suggested that the best way to deal with this is just to re-cut the songs… and also, I said, this will mean for every album that we're doing, you already have three or four songs before you even start."

Thus, all of The Wailers' early albums have new licks of old tunes. The new versions are slightly more sophisticated with higher production values, but, at the end of the day, they are not always necessarily "better" than the originals.

The unison lead vocal of 'Put It On' was mixed with Marley's voice higher in the mix than Bunny's and Peter's, but it's clear that at this point in the recording of the album all three still had significant creative and vocal input.

THE WAILERS' OWN TUFF GONG RECORD SHOP.

SMALL AXE

Marley's reminder to his Trench Town constituents that all power is not vested in the establishment; the little man has more power than he realizes.

57

So, too, does a little nation. As Jamaicans say, "Wi lickle but wi tallewah" (small but strong).

The lyrics to 'Small Axe' have also been said to allude to what were then the island's "Big Three" ("free") main distributors – Dynamics, Federal and Studio One – and The Wailers' determination to find their own niche in the marketing end of the business. It was a mission they successfully managed to accomplish: the Jamaican music industry is still ruled by a three-pronged monopoly, but two of the players have changed. Dynamics (owned by soca bandleader, Chinese-Jamaican Byron Lee) now competes with Sonic Sounds (founded by Byron Lee's brother, Neville) and The Wailers' own Tuff Gong.

Originally recorded at Randy's Studio in 1969, 'Small Axe' was the third tune to be re-cut for Island, a move not only good for the group but good for the label's gaffer.

RASTAMAN CHANT

Rastaman Chant' is more likely to be heard at a Nyabingi (Rasta retreat) than on a pop music album, but such was the power of The Wailers that they could take what is essentially a religious hymn and make it cool enough for secular consumption.

The percussion pattern on 'Rastaman Chant', played by Bunny Wailer, is the traditional drum beat of Rastafari, the call to arms for Jah children that keeps Nyabingi drummers going through a long night of reasoning and passing of the chillum pipe.

A Nyabingi (the word interpreted by some Rastas as meaning "death to all black and white oppressors", and by others to mean an "irie" gathering) is similar in intent to a religious service, but one which is also an extended (sometimes for several days) social gathering of the island's numerous Rasta clans who take turns hosting the Nyabingi camp. Outsiders are welcome if invited (and after being carefully screened). It is wise to arrive (and leave) accompanied by a respected Rasta bredren, and it is also wise not to try to keep up with the indigenous smokers, some of whom can put away a seven-inch spliff and still carry on an intelligent conversation.

DUPPY CONQUEROR

Another of The Wailers' re-cut originals, and once again with the undeniable input of Chris Blackwell giving the track the sophisticated

"I DROPPED THE 'BOB MARLEY' FOR THE FIRST TWO RECORDS SO THEY WOULD HAVE A GROUP IMAGE."
CHRIS BLACKWELL

edge lacking on the original cut. This was all-important if Blackwell was to achieve his aim of placing the band – and, increasingly, Bob Marley – on the international market.

Says Blackwell of his marketing strategy: "I wanted to position them as a black group, rather than a reggae act, because reggae acts in general, other than perhaps a Jimmy Cliff, were novelty acts. There was always a reggae hit every year, but it was usually a different artist… it wasn't music that was considered serious musicianship, so I felt that Bob should be presented as a black group – like there was War at that time, or Earth Wind And Fire, or Sly & The Family Stone, black groups which were given a kind of rock sensibility, and I felt that *that* was what Bob Marley And The Wailers – or really The Wailers, because I dropped the 'Bob Marley' for the first two records so they would have a group image – should be marketed as."

NATTY DREAD

1975

PRODUCED BY CHRIS BLACKWELL AND THE WAILERS

NO WOMAN NO CRY

REVOLUTION

NATTY DREAD

TALKIN' BLUES

THEM BELLY FULL (BUT WE HUNGRY)

LIVELY UP YOURSELF

REBEL MUSIC (3 O'CLOCK ROADBLOCK)

SO JAH SEY

"The *Natty Dread* album is like one step more forward for reggae music. Betta music, betta lyrics… it have a betta feelin'. *Catch A Fire* and *Burnin'* have a good feelin', but *Natty Dread* is improved." So did a satisfied Bob Marley sum up his newly completed album in 1974. The third album for Island Records, and the first for Bob as a solo act, it was released to great critical fanfare in February, 1975.

Like its two predecessors, *Natty Dread* was recorded at Harry J's studio. After laying the bed tracks, Family Man remembers that recording was interrupted by an invitation from Taj Mahal to go to California to help mix the 'Mu' Roots album. "Bob accepted and four of us – me, Bob, Alan 'Skill' Cole, and Lee Jaffee. Taj Mahal (one of the first international artists to experiment with reggae) did over 'Slave Driver', too."

While in the United States, Family Man Barrett listened intently to the music on local radio stations, seeking sounds that he could incorporate into The Wailers' music. "I listened to Curtis Mayfield (also a favourite of Marley's), Chaka Khan, JJ Cale… but I especially listened to James Brown, yeah, James Brown's 'The Payback'. When I heard that I said to myself, 'This is what we're gonna be don' on *Natty Dread*."

Marley and his Wailers band did the *Natty Dread* overdubs in London, at Island's Basing Street Studio, where American guitarist Al Anderson was recruited, and once again the end result convinced Blackwell to continue backing Bob even though Island had not yet started to recoup the estimated half-million dollars invested. "People read that they're the greatest thing since sliced bread," notes the man who has been critical to the career of many of pop music's better acts, "but they haven't actually got

THE ORIGINAL NATTY DREAD, HIS NATTY IN ONE OF THE KNITTED TAMS THAT EVERY SELF-RESPECTING RASTAMAN WORE IN THE SEVENTIES.

any money coming in. So I would advance royalties to Bob that he hadn't really earned." The key to both bringing in some money, and attracting a wider audience was, Blackwell believed, touring. "Bob's success came from people seeing him and saying, 'Fuck, I can't believe this guy; and then going and buying the record." Bob Marley, however; was not an easy man to get back on the road after the early tours turned sour. In fact, some of the executives at Island were getting a little edgy. It was at this critical juncture that Don Taylor began to manage the rising reggae star.

"One good thing I have to say about Don Taylor," says Chris Blackwell – talking about a man about whom he has very few good things to say – "he was able to get Bob on the road."

Taylor, for once, agrees with Blackwell's version of events: "Yes, it was definitely me who got him to go out on tour."

Don Taylor, like Bob grew up on the streets of downtown Kingston and, in his words, began hustling at a very young age. He perfected his technique, he confides, on easily-conned cruise ship passengers (a hustling tradition still practised today).

"I was," he says, "all things to all persons… tour guide, pimp or hustler." His transition from working the streets to working behind the scenes in the entertainment business happened when Taylor, who had been providing a personal valet service to visiting R&B singers, accepted Jerry Butler's offer to join his tour as his valet, a break from which he parlayed into an extended stint as manager of black acts like Little Anthony and The Imperials.

Taylor's street skills served him well in the tricky, tough and Mob-riddled world of American music of which he was now a part. By the time he approached Bob Marley with his offer to manage him, Taylor had paid his dues and knew what he was doing. Marley, sensing that Taylor had considerably more "smarts" than anyone else within Kingston's thriving but unsophisticated music world, agreed that Taylor could join his team.

One of the first things Taylor did was renegotiate The Wailers' contract with Island. Having quickly realized that the existing agreement had been nullified with the departure of two of the three signatories, and he considered that a new one signed by Bob Marley was also of dubious legal standing, Taylor used the situation to his advantage, raising the bottom line from what Jamaicans call "sweetie money" to a decent deal, which included the bargain $250,000 purchase of Blackwell's 56 Hope Road house where Bob had already been living for a couple of years, and which nowadays houses a rudimentary "museum" showcasing an unim-

"ME REALLY LOVE 'NO WOMAN NO CRY' BECAUSE IT MEANS SO MUCH TO ME. SO MUCH FEELING ME GET FROM IT. REALLY LOVE IT."
BOB MARLEY

'No Woman No Cry' was released as a single in Great Britain and stayed in the charts for seven weeks, rising at one point to Number 20. Remarkably, in 1981, shortly after Marley's demise, it re-entered that same chart, this time peaking at Number 8.

The superb live version of the song (that appears on *Live!*) was recorded at The Roxy in LA. It comes up in conversation with Chris Blackwell when he is asked what his most memorable moment with Bob was. "There were so many," he answers, "but I'll give you one." He looks straight ahead at the still, sapphire green sea that fronts his GoldenEye property. "It was at The Roxy. It was the first time I heard the audience sing along with 'NWNC', and I thought, 'if we could get a live record with the audience singing along' – it had such an incredible atmosphere. That's when I decided to put out a live album."

REVOLUTION

On April 14, 1999, the PNP finance minister, Omar Davies, announced in the budget, a whopping 31 per cent increase in the price of petrol (which translated at the pumps to about US$1.00 jump per gallon). There was, he said, no alternative. Over the following few days, the country was crippled by hundreds of random roadblocks. "Nation Ablaze" is the theme of CVM Television's nightly news as fires burn everywhere. Crudely-made cardboard picket signs saying "PJ (Prime Minister Patterson) must go", "The people cyaan tek no more", and "Revolution is a must" were waved from every

MARLEY ARRIVES FOR A 1974 SHOW AT THE BIRMINGHAM ODEON ON THE *NATTY DREAD* TOUR.

street corner, and for the first time in the nation's history, the middle classes were out in full support of the poor.

Thirty-five years after 'Revolution was released, its relevance is stronger than ever. Bob Marley is, once again (in Stevie Wonder's words) "hot on the box", and this persuasive call to arms is one of the favoured songs of the day, another being the contrasting universal plea for peace, 'One Love'.

After three days of chaos, the riots ended with the government's pledge to "roll back" the gas tax 50 per cent, a move that stopped the violence, but was greeted with scepticism by many who questioned Patterson's ability to perform the function of prime minister and who now rated him as Jamaica's most unpopular head of government ever.

In 1974, Marley's reference to revolution was of far different origin. Michael Manley's Democratic Socialist government was intent on forging an alliance with Fidel Castro's communist Cuba, and, initially, the poor of Jamaica thought this to be a good thing, worthy of a revolution. After a short time in office Manley's credibility was eroding even among his core supporters. "Joshua" (his Biblical nickname) was seen to have flaws and Marley, who had once courted politicians on both sides, began to distance himself from the system. 'Revolution' was his first open reference to his disillusionment. "Never make a politician grant you a favour, they will want to control you for ever", was a warning gleaned from personal experience.

NATTY DREAD

This song was first released as 'Knotty Dread', as dreadlocksed youths were first known. ("Natty" would come into the language from the Jamaican pronunciation of "knotty".)

Initially, the popularity of dreadlocks seemed synonymous with the increase in the popularity of the hair-style's most influential wearer. As Marley told Third World's Ibo Cooper when he came back from an early tour, "The whole a Jamaica full a Bob Marleys." But the sudden spread of locks didn't make them any more socially acceptable. Those of Marley's children who had sported locks (like Ziggy) were forced to trim before being accepted at the strict uptown schools they attended in the Eighties. It was not until they were out of school and independent that they could dread.

In the Nineties, school rules have relaxed greatly and most schools now allow the dreadlocksed children of Rastas to attend as long as their

ZIGGY MARLEY
DIDN'T START
'LOCKING' UNTIL HE
LEFT ARDENNE HIGH
SCHOOL.

locks are contained by caps. But discrimination against "nattier" still exists. Unless famous or wealthy, those who "locks" are still perceived as socially inferior by the uptown "verandah set", a perception not helped by the fact that the island's street population of "mad men" are (solely by reason of not cutting their hair) naturally natty, nor by the reality that many who dread are, in the Jamaican parlance, more "rascal" than Rasta.

TALKIN' BLUES

The rebel with many causes said that the line was not to be taken literally, but the violent sentiment expressed by Marley in 'Talkin' Blues' – "I feel like burning a church now" – has continued to draw criticism. If Bob Marley was indeed a man of peace, the question is asked, how could he possibly sing of bombs (or even of revolution)? But the very complex character that was Bob Marley answered this himself: "I don't come down on you really with blood and fire, earth-quake and lightning, but you must know seh that within me all a that exists." And 'Talkin' Blues' is one of the best examples of how Marley's music always tempered the tart message with a sweet melody.

'Talkin' Blues' (though credited solely to Carlton Family Man Barrett) probably had its origins in Marley's brief association with his father. Recounting that Mr Marley Sr habitually spoke of "stones for my pillow and the sky is my roof" (during what she describes as his "frequent weepy moods"), Cedella Booker believes that her son's "cold ground was my bed last night, rock stone was my pillow", spoken of in 'Talkin' Blues' came directly from his father's frequent lament.

THEM BELLY FULL (BUT WE HUNGRY)

The original Island tracksheet for 'Them Belly Full (But We Hungry)' gives an illustration of the increasing musical complexity of The Wailers' music from 2-track to 16-track and now, on *Natty Dread*, to 24-track. The sheet shows that Al Anderson overdubbed two lead guitar tracks on this song, and that tracks 10 and 22 had tenor sax parts. (In fact, Chris Blackwell believed that Bob's music was better off without the horn sound: "I just didn't like it," he says, pointing out that if nothing else it created a logistical problem on tour – "more plane tickets, more hotel rooms".)

Of the lyrics, when interviewed Marley said: "Your belly's full, but we're hungry for the love of our brethren. Food might be in your belly, but there's more to living than just filling it. Where's the love of your brother?" Or, as Family Man puts it, the song is about "trying to feed the multitude with just a handful of corn."

During the 1999 riots, the song's perennial relevance would hit home again. "The people are hungry," said JLP Member of Parliament, Babsy Grange, letting her large audience at a women's peace rally (called in an attempt to end the turmoil) finish off the thought themselves… "and a hungry man is an angry man".

LIVELY UP YOURSELF

Written as 'Liven Up Yourself' on the original Island track-sheet (perhaps a grammatical correction of the Jamaican vernacular), this song ventured over the familiar 16-track line to 18, but then Track 17, a second backing

"SOOTHE (THE WARRING INSTINCTS) OF THE SAVAGE BEAST."
BOB MARLEY

vocals track, was crossed out. An engineer's note on Track I (organ) reads, "keep low", and, as on 'Them Belly Full', two extra guitar tracks have been overdubbed by Al Anderson.

This is one of Marley's "irie vibes" songs, frequently dropped in by the artist, says former Marley art director Neville Garrick, "to get the crowd moving during stageshows" (a ploy Prince would copy with his cover of the song in the mid-Eighties). "They would drop it in," Garrick says, "and send Junior Marvin (often called the 'second star' by the press) out there."

'Lively Up Yourself' is still a crowd-pleaser when covered, as it often is, by other reggae bands. A paean to the power of reggae music and its ability to lift the most oppressed of spirits, and "soothe (the warring instincts of) the savage beast", 'Lively Up Yourself' is another Wailers' song pulled back into public consciousness in the tense days that follow the April, 1999 rioting.

REBEL MUSIC

Throughout the Seventies and Eighties, police and Army roadblocks were commonplace. To be stopped by soldiers in full military garb, and to be harassed for no reason, was almost a certainty, especially when driving from town to town. 'Rebel Music' was based on a real roadblock Marley encountered while driving across the island with his then girlfriend, Esther Anderson the photographer responsible for the covers of both *Catch A Fire* and *Burnin'* (and one-time love interest of Chris Blackwell).

Called 'Roadblock' more often than by its correct title, this song is Don Taylor's favourite, because, he says, it tells a story not just about a roadblock, but of the ghetto child's life: there is always something trying to block you.

Whether it was the people who took the road-block idea from the police or vice versa, the blocking of roads by the island's citizens is now a well-entrenched Jamaican tradition (dating back at least to the Sixties, and, some old-time Jamaicans say, the Forties).

Roadblocks are the people's way of dealing with any real or perceived injustice and, traditionally, too often the only way the government pays any attention to its constituents' complaints. Using anything at hand – tyres, trees, rocks, car wrecks and cast-off appliances (which are all set on fire), roadblocks can create havoc, and not infrequently create additional income for the perpetrators who will allow safe passage in exchange for a "pass" fee.

BOB MARLEY LIVE
IN 1980.

"YOUR BELLY'S
FULL, BUT WE'RE
HUNGRY FOR THE
LOVE OF OUR
BRETHREN. FOOD
MIGHT BE IN
YOUR BELLY BUT
THERE'S MORE TO
LIVING THAN JUST
FILLING IT."
BOB MARLEY

SO JAH SEY

Officially credited to Will Francisco and Rita Anderson (Marley), 'So Jah Sey' is another of the songs that Don Taylor says he "picked (writers') names at random", but the tune bears Marley's unmistakable lyrical cadence and content a combination of Biblical phrase, Jamaican proverb, patois colour and pop hooks.

Neither Rita, nor any of Marley's "seeds" will ever have to sit "in the sidewalk and beg bread", as he states in the song, since five of his 11 offspring (legitimate and otherwise) got a million dollar settlement from his estate and the rest remain as beneficiaries. Prior to this point, though, says Don Taylor among others, some of the Gong's illegitimate children went without support for several years. "If my only crime was to make Rita accountable to the outside children, then I'm happy I did it," says Taylor, answering a question about the negative way many in the Marley camp perceive him. "I said it was unfair that these children weren't getting funds some of them were only getting JA$80.00 a week and I was called in to expose this by Mrs Booker (who had adopted Rohan, one of the illegitimate heirs)."

Only three of Bob's children were borne by Rita. The others – Rohan, Julian, Robbie, Kymani, Karen, Damian, and Makada – came courtesy of a total of seven "baby mothers". Also acknowledged as an heir to the estate was Stephanie, Rita Marley's daughter by a man named Ital.

ZIGGY MARLEY WITH HIS SISTERS – CEDELLA FAR RIGHT AND SHARON AT THE BACK, REACHING FOR THE BABY.

RASTAMAN VIBRATION

An album that was, according to Chris Blackwell, "a conscious attempt to break into the black American market", *Rastaman Vibration* was released during a year of political chaos in Jamaica that, from Marley's perspective, began with the death of a step-father he had grown to love, and ended with a botched attempt by gunmen on his own life. Two days later, he appeared at a free concert for the people – *Smile Jamaica* – in downtown Kingston.

Bob Marley, whose idea it had been to do the benefit show, did not want *Smile Jamaica* to be politicized, but Michael Manley had other plans. A couple of days after the prime minister had approved the concept, and Marley had announced the show, Manley held his own press conference where he announced the date of the next election – timed shortly after the concert. Bob Marley was angered by Manley's crafty political move, but chose neither to cancel nor postpone the free show for the people. Then came the shoot-out at his Hope Road home.

Speculation about whether or not Marley would brave the stage at the *Smile Jamaica* event (which would become one of the two milestone local concerts of his career) ended when the red vehicle that had carried him, under armed guard, from his Blue Mountain hide-away, pulled up backstage. Still-bandaged, the singer took to the stage and, after hugging a beaming Michael Manley, addressed an emotionally explosive audience of about 50,000 people with the stirring and appropriate words of 'War'.

Like all election years in Jamrock, 1976 was marked by the kind of senseless violence that serves, on this very controlled island, only to maintain the political status quo. On June 19, the Governor General, or "GG", Sir Florizel Glasspole, declared a State of Emergency to combat what incumbent Prime Minister

BOB MARLEY IN
HAPPY MOOD,
GLOUCESTER ROAD,
LONDON, 1978.

Michael Manley saw as a joint plot by opposition leader Edward Seaga, and the United States' CIA, to discredit his party. Caught in the middle, Marley was increasingly seen as supporting Manley's People's National Party (PNP), a suspected allegiance which many feel was the reason he almost died on the night of December 3, when two car-loads of gunmen broke into the grounds of 56 Hope Road, and shot the singer, wife Rita, and manager Don Taylor – who took five of the bullets meant for Bob, and whose legs, crossed as he sits on the cream-coloured couch in his living room, a mere stone's throw from where he was shot, still bear the jagged scars of that night.

As it was later told, Marley had just taken a rehearsal break and was eating a grapefruit when the first shot was fired. Taylor crossed the room in the line of fire, sparing Marley all but one of the shots intended for him. Rita Marley was hit in the head when she stepped out from her yellow Volkswagen to investigate the noise that everyone initially thought had come from fireworks, while The Wailers, so the story goes, took shelter in the bathtub.

Nancy Burke, a friend of both Cindy Breakespeare and Marley, was on her way to Hope Road and heard the shots as she approached the property. Turning into the gates, minutes after the gunmen had fled, she describes the scene as ominous. "There was total silence," she says. "I thought everyone had been massacred."

The injured trio were quickly taken north up Hope Road to the University Hospital, following which Marley, released as soon as his minor wound was dressed, was moved up the adjacent mountain to Chris Blackwell's isolated Strawberry Hill estate in Irish Town. Marley later said, "Them come through the door and start shoot, blood claat. Dat mean me cyaan move. One time I move to one side, and the gun shot flew over deh… the feel-in' I had was to run hard but God jus' move mi in time. His Majesty was directing me and as me move me feel like I get high… I tell yuh, Rasta dangerous."

Third World, the opening act on *Smile Jamaica*, decided, despite understandable misgivings, to do the show as scheduled. Ibo Cooper, the group's keyboardist, remembers that Marley called him at home "every five minutes" for Cooper to confirm that he was leaving his house for the venue. "He would not rest until I said I was leaving my yard" When Third World started to play before a "peaceful but excited" crowd, it was obvious, says Cooper, "that the people wanted Bob". Given a radio by the show's producer and asked to call Marley, Cooper says that "only then did Bob finally decide to come".

*"RASTAMAN
VIBRATION
GONNA COVER
THE EARTH LIKE
THE WATER
COVER THE SEA."*
BOB MARLEY

Cat Coore remembers being told that Marley, accompanied by a heavy police escort, came down Gordon Town Road (a very narrow and dangerous mountain road) at full speed, arriving at the venue just as Third World's set finished.

Some of The Wailers decided not to play. "Some of Third World stood in for them," recalls Cooper, "but then, as the music took over, one by one The Wailers started to come onstage, pick up a bass, or a guitar and begin to play". The set continued with a mix of musicians from both bands. "The song list was spontaneous," Cooper says. "Bob would call each song in the middle of the song before it, and every song somehow fit together… it was like he was telling a story, chapter by chapter." As for the singer, "he was in another world, transported somewhere far beyond the stage," delivering his militant message in his usual peaceful and mesmerising style. After the show, the huge crowd surprised the cynics by dispersing quietly.

In the end, Michael Manley's political manouvering seemed to work. As Cat Coore concluded: *"Smile Jamaica* sealed the election."

Rastaman Vibration was the perfect release for this tumultuous year. It was an album that reflected Marley's growing belief in the peaceful philosophy of Rastafarianism and his new alliance with the Twelve Tribes of Israel (the likely result of the many nights spent "reasoning" with the elders in Rasta-dominated Bull Bay). Sporting a burlap-like sleeve, designed by Neville Garrick after The Skipper, pointing to a piece of burlap which had a photo leaning against it had said "album design dat" (and which the liner notes suggested could double as a cutting board for cleaning herb), *Rastaman Vibration* went immediately into the Top 10 in Britain and was an even bigger seller in the US, peaking at Number 8, proving that the minstrel from the Tribe of Judah had delivered a hip message for the times.

The December election result surprised no one. Just as Bob Marley was the musician for those troubled times, Manley was the politician with the power to pull the people behind him as no other before him. Not even his father, the revered Norman Manley, founder of the party his son had just led to his second victory, could come close to the reverence accorded to Michael.

Tall, elegant of manner, but able to touch the people on such a visceral level that the Promised Land was not only a viable possibility, but with "Joshua" leading them, a distinct probability. With his "rod of correction" held high, Michael's authority was absolute, and the people were wild with hope for a future in which they would have a say. All of this despite a first four-year term in office that had been a frightening failure.

With a commitment to the citizens of Jamaica that he would never, ever begin to fulfil, Manley's reign began with the belief that Jamaica was at long last coming into its own, and continued in 1976 with the fallacy that it was just taking a little longer. Middle-class sceptics saw the situation a little more clearly, and the flights out of Jamaica continued, filled with disillusioned emigrants.

Bob Marley's departure from his home a few months earlier, shaken and very grateful to be alive, had a profound effect on his work. As Errol Browne says: "After the shooting, his lyrics got more serious."

WAR

Putting the powerful words of Emperor Haile Selassie, King of Kings, Conquering Lion of the Tribe of Judah, to music was Marley intimate Alan "Skill" Cole's idea. Originally delivered to the United Nations in 1968, Selassie's passionate plea for human rights acquires additional power when poetically edited by Marley, and accompanied by the insistent drive of drum and bass. Although he wasn't given a writer's credit, Selassie's spirit lives on in this song, for who among those familiar with the opening bars can ever ignore the truth in the words: "Until the philosophy which holds one race superior… and another… inferior… is finally… and permanently… discredited… and abandoned. Everywhere is war."

War was on everyone's lips in the Jamaica of the mid-Seventies. With tourism at an all-time low (middle America, and even the more adventurous Europeans scared away by the escalating violence), and the guns that were normally confined to the ghetto finding their way into more and more uptown areas, the middle classes of Jamaica were fleeing by the hundreds. Manley, who saw this mass migration as being akin to treason, encouraged the exodus, telling the unfaithful departing to hurry "get their seat" on one of the numerous daily flights to Miami.

JOHNNY WAS

Popularly believed to be about Carlton "Batman" Wilson, brother of singer Dellrow Wilson, it seems more likely that the lyrics of 'Johnny Was' are intended simply to pay tribute to the thousands of ghetto "yout'" shot down by "stray" bullets on the divided Kingston streets over the past 40 years, and the mothers who have cried so much that they are said to have no more tears left to shed.

EXODUS

1977

*PRODUCED BY BOB MARLEY
AND THE WAILERS*

THREE LITTLE BIRDS

WAITING IN VAIN

TURN YOUR LIGHTS DOWN LOW

ONE LOVE

NATURAL MYSTIC

JAMMING

EXODUS

GUILTINESS

THE HEATHEN

SO MUCH THINGS TO SAY

DREAD TAKES A DRAW OUTSIDE THE GATES OF MARLEY'S SPECTACULAR BUT NEVER-COMPLETED STUDIO COMPLEX AT FORT MARIA.

The *Natty Dread* tour – Bob's solo debut – was a huge success for the man so many were hailing as not only the king of reggae music, but also the hottest new thing in rock.

That Marley crossed over the line that had always kept reggae acts locked firmly in the ethnic closet, and was now so appealing to the fickle rock audience was largely down to Chris Blackwell. He believed firmly that a good producer will always have a marketing plan even before going into the studio. "From the outset," he says, "whatever I did was always with a thought to marketing." He continues: "This is why I brought in Wayne (Perkins) and Rabbit for the overdubs on *Catch A Fire*. I planned to hit with the rock sound, to open up the market. We could then pull back to a more simple (or raw) sound, but first we had to get in the door."

Just before *Exodus* was released in May of 1977, Bob Marley and Family Man Barrett were charged in a London court with possession of ganja, but were both let off with a light fine (£50 and £20, respectively), and a lecture from a slightly bemused judge. This was one of the very rare instances that herb's biggest promoter was actually held accountable for his open smoking and tireless crusade for the legalization of weed. "The more people smoke, the more Babylon fall," was his fervent belief.

Exodus, the fifth studio album for Island Records, had as much of a rock influence as the group's first LP for the label and drew additional criticism for being too sophisticated, too international, too far away from Marley's roots (a cardinal sin for reggae musicians). But this particular reggae musician, as always, had a perfect comeback: "Marley's music is always Marley's music. I haven't changed my musical sound. A man plays his music according to the way he feels." What had changed, however, were his musicians. Tyrone Downie, who had been raised "with differing music all around me, the church on one side, a sound system on the other" and with Peter Tosh as his neighbour, had a very open mind to new sounds, and he began to take over some of the arranging from the more conservative Family Man. Furthermore, in the wake of Al Anderson's departure to play with Peter Tosh's Word, Sound And Power, Junior Marvin was hired.

Marvin, a Jamaican-born British guitarist with a post-Hendrix pop sound brought with him a European sensibility as opposed to the American input of Perkins and Anderson. Impressed by Marley's professionalism, Marvin was immediately made aware by the group's leader he was expected to follow his strict example.

In retrospect, *Exodus* sounds as roots reggae as it comes, and is perhaps the album where all of his many sides worked together for the first time. In the disco-happy Seventies, however, the music on this set was considered radical, a quality that could have been the reason why the elusive black audience Marley had been courting since the Sixties suddenly started to listen. It was the title track of *Exodus*, which, with its urgent Afrocentric lyrics, was added to R&B playlists and which, when released as a single, was bought in large numbers by the black community.

The small but growing interest of the hard-to-crack R&B audience was helped greatly by the interest and support of Stevie Wonder, who was so drawn to reggae that in the early Eighties he moved into the Intercontinental Hotel in Ocho Rios for several months, taking the hotel's resident reggae band, Happiness Unlimited, back to California with him when he left. Wonder developed a relationship with Marley and performed with him on at least two occasions. His tribute song to his friend, 'Master Blaster Jammin'' is not only an acknowledgement of Marley's power, but a prophetic hint that one day the blacks of both Jamaica and the USA would unite through music.

The Bob Marley And The Wailers tour of continental Europe started as soon as *Exodus* hit the streets, and its success was duplicated in a series of dates at North London's Rainbow Theatre. Momentum was picking up daily – Jamaican artist, Nancy Burke, who was part of Marley's London entourage, describes it as "an energy so intense it seemed it would never end". But a problem suddenly emerged that would bring this phenomenon to a close – and much sooner than anyone could have imagined.

In 1975, Marley had injured his toe playing football. Asked about it in 1977 he said, "In Paris, I was playing soccer and a man gave me a rasclaat tackle in the rain. The foot started paining me and I wonder… why it burn for so long. I score a goal and just hop off the field. When I took off my shoe, the toenail was completely out."

Ignoring medical advice at the time to refrain from further football, Marley continued indulging in his second most important passion. Staying in London's Oakley Street, a location picked especially because of its close proximity to soccer-friendly Battersea Park, Marley made the game a part of his daily routine. During one of these casual matches, another skirmish with a player resulted in his toe being further injured by his opponent's rusty cleats. Again, Marley kept on kicking, giving the toe no chance to heal.

On July 7, 1977, a day foretold in Rasta theology to be the "Two Sevens Clash", or a day of serious import, Denise Mills took Bob to a Harley Street specialist. (Mills who, after single-handedly running Island's Jamaican affairs from her vine-covered, white cottage overlooking Ocho Rios Bay for many years, would herself die at a young age from emphysema in 1995.) She remained reluctant to talk about Bob's illness, even after several years had elapsed since his death. But she did say that no one – least of all she and Bob – had any inkling on that hot July day that the toe would not be easily treated.

The British doctor recommended amputation, but Marley, thinking he would have difficulty performing without the toe, opted instead to cancel the US leg of his tour, fly to Miami and live in a newly-purchased villa with his mother for five months. He also consulted another doctor while in Florida who told him that a skin graft would save the toe.

In a fateful decision, Marley opted for the less drastic solution. It was a decision that would ultimately cost him his life.

THREE LITTLE BIRDS

On one of Kingston's main thoroughfares sits 56 Hope Road, in a good residential area of town, full of fruit trees, flowers and birds. Written on the back step of Hope Road, where Marley sat for many an hour picking out tunes on his guitar, and trying out lyrics ("It used to sound like gibberish at first," says Cindy Breakespeare, "but he'd sing it over and over and words would begin to come."). 'Three Little Birds' is believed to have been inspired by three small ground doves that would hang out by Bob's doorstep. The birds were attracted by the steady supply of seeds discarded during the ritual of herb cleaning, which, for the Rastaman, is almost as important as the rolling of the spliff and the sacramental smoking of the holy herb.

Almost certainly the inspiration for Bobby McFerrin's Eighties hit, 'Don't Worry', 'Three Little Birds', with its simple advice and reassurance ("Don't worry about a thing, 'cos every little thing's gonna be OK") has

helped many a despondent ghetto dweller through another hard Jamaican day, and become a staple of the now almost extinct three-man calypso groups which, with their homemade rhythm boxes, maracas, and acoustic guitars were once such an integral part of the tourist experience.

WAITING IN VAIN

Arguably Marley's best and most played love song (vying only with 'Could You Be Loved?' for top spot), 'Waiting In Vain' begs the question, Who was it written for?" (Don Taylor says that Cindy Breakespeare – before she became Bob's girl – was the elusive woman he didn't want to waste time on, but it's not one of the songs she takes inspirational credit for), and the soulful vocal of a man so intrigued by the chase that the capture has to be a letdown, never fails to affect the listener because of its wistful honesty.

"Women were always throwing themselves at his feet," says Cindy Breakespeare, who despite her long and close relationship with the singer was described by him as "one of my girlfriends". Breakespeare, early on, adopted the policy of "giving him his space", and it was a space that was rarely vacant. From pauper to princess, Marley had them all. Yet it was only Rita Marley who captured, and kept, the post of his legal "queen".

Like most Rastamen, Marley was attracted to the women of "Babylon", those who wore makeup and dressed in jeans and minidresses. But he was also true to his Rasta faith in that he would admonish his women that a bare face was beautiful, and a frock far more in keeping with women's rightful role. Keeping women barefoot, pregnant and in the

"I USED TO SOUND LIKE GIBBERISH AT FIRST, BUT HE'D SING IT OVER AND OVER AND WORDS WOULD BEGIN TO COME." CINDY BREAKSPEARE

kitchen (except when menstruating, at which time women are required to keep their distance from all food preparation) is a practiced principle of Rasta doctrine. "I had to ask if I was ready to throw away my razor and nail polish," says Breakespeare, who also remembers trying unsuccessfully to hide the fact that she wore makeup from her musician boyfriend.

Who Marley was yearning for in this song will never be known, but as his wife, Rita, ruefully recalls that, "Bob loved to be seen as a lover, not just as a rebel."

TURN YOUR LIGHTS DOWN LOW

On a sunny January morning, Cindy Breakespeare sits sipping strong coffee in the eclectic and charming Stony Hill apartment. "'Turn Your Lights Down Low' was written for me at Hope Road," she confides. Breakespeare, looking, in her long cotton print dress with face free of make-up, very much in synch with Rasta dress codes, admits that it was initially hard for her to consider dating a dread. Having attended Immaculate Conception High School – still considered the best of the Kingston's many all-girl secondary schools, and so "proper" that its students wear

RITA MARLEY IN 1982, ONE YEAR AFTER HER HUSBAND'S DEATH.

petticoats under their white uniforms – she was taught, in the Rastaphobic Seventies, that if an Immaculate girl saw a Rastaman coming towards them they were to cross the road and "keep our eyes straight ahead". "Rastaman were said to be mad," she says. It's not surprising that Cindy Breakespeare found the forbidden enticing. "It was a very exciting time in Jamaica for those who understood the Rasta culture." For those who didn't, it was very threatening.

In its beginning, the Rasta philosophy was very seductive and, as its foremost practitioner, Bob Marley was a master seducer. Whatever the topic, his music seduced. It pulled you in and held you spellbound – a positive alternative to a largely negative world.' Turn Your Lights Down Low' is a lighter example of Marley's musical might, but shows how powerful a simple love song can be.

ONE LOVE

Being a "relic" of the original Coxsone Dodd track, this is the work that most embodies the message of Bob Marley: One love, one heart, let's get together and feel all right". And although Jamaica's official national anthem is 'Jamaica Land We Love', it is 'One Love' that the world sings when it wants to make a point. The title has also made its way into the Jamaican language as a righteous way to greet or leave someone.

Sadly, the "one love" sentiment that proved so magnetic to Marley's followers seems to have passed on with its creator. The modern Rasta is more intent on burning down than building bridges, and the original "one love" dread is becoming an endangered species as the militant Bobo dreads take control of the faith. The Bobos, a sub-sect of Rastafari whose members believe in confining their locks under tight turbans as much as the Rastas of the Seventies and Eighties believed in flashing them, and who preach insurrection as much as Marley preached love, were once confined to a very small community in Bull Bay (a few miles outside Kingston where Bob Marley once housed his wife and children). Traditionally supporting themselves by selling handmade brooms at busy Kingston intersections, as well as door-to-door, the Bobos have diversified of late into the more lucrative entertainment business, and have led the Rasta movement since the mid-Nineties, creating a rift between them and other branches of the faith.

"Unity is the world's key to racial harmony," said Marley "Until the white man stops calling himself white, and the black man stops calling himself black, we will not see it. All the people on earth are just one family." He also made clear that "Me don' dip on the black man's side, nor the white man's side, me dip on God's side."

In the years since the reggae bard's death, 'One Love' has been used extensively by the Jamaica Tourist Board to sell Jamaica in prime-time ads on CNN. The high-budget commercial presents Jamaica as a land of love, peace and harmony. "Out of many one people" is indeed the island's motto, but it is an ideal still waiting to be realized.

"ME DON' DIP ON THE BLACK MAN'S SIDE NOR WHITE MAN'S SIDE, ME DIP ON GOD'S SIDE."
BOB MARLEY

PRODUCER CLEMENT 'SIR COXSONE' DODD, WHOSE STUDIO ONE LABEL WAS RESPONSIBLE FOR 'SIMMER DOWN', THE WAILERS' FIRST HIT IN 1964.

Marley recorded several other versions of 'One Love', including a 12-inch remix which fused into the original recording parts of Curtis Mayfeld's 'People Get Ready' to emphasize the song's plea.

NATURAL MYSTIC

Perry Henzell, director of the cult classic, *The Harder They Come*, once said of Jamaica that its mysterious energy is the result of the island being a "red hot" connector between the cultures of Africa and North America, and anyone who has felt this energy's presence can vouch for its existence. Surrender to it and it will take you on a journey you'll never forget. Marley called this phenomenon the "natural mystic", but the song may also have had a more personal interpretation. "I believe he was the 'natural mystic'. I think he was singing about himself" posits Cindy Breakespeare, who names this track as her favourite – "Whenever I hear it, it makes me feel a way."

EDWARD SEAGA, PRIME MINISTER OF JAMAICA FROM 1980 TO 1988, AND EARLY RECORD PRODUCER.

Jamaica's spiritual centre is a complex mix of Pocomania, Pentecostal, Catholicism, Anglican and Rastafari, and when these elements converge strange things happen, none of which really can be explained. "Those who feel it, know it," is Rita Marley's explanation. Dave Tollington, senior vice president of Warner Music, and former disc jock at Toronto's groundbreaking radio station, CHUM-FM, who remembers clearly being rooted to the spot the first time he heard Bob Marley in the mid-Seventies, and who has made countless pilgrimages to Jamaica since then, and Sting, who wrote many of the songs on his *The Dream Of The Blue Turtles* album in Jamaica, also claims to have felt the vibe.

JAMMING

It has often been said that it is the poor that bear the burden of keeping Jamaica afloat. Other classes may have suffered increased hardship as the country's economy drifts closer and closer on its sea of corruption to complete bankruptcy, but it is the "massive" who suffer the most.

95

"We are the living sacrifice," sang the man who, although he had now moved to a much more up-market address, never really left the ghetto, "and we're jammin' right straight from yard", in a song that unites the two main components of his music—joy and Jah. Released in a 12-inch version that was a 1977 club hit, 'Jamming' is one of those rare songs with a religious theme that is also hailed as great dance record. 'Jamming' was also the song that the Gong was singing when he called upon the warring politicians Michael Manley and Edward Seaga to join him onstage and shake hands during the memorable *One Love* concert – a moment replayed in the minds of many Jamaicans when Seaga (who would go on to become prime minister from 1980-1988 before, once again, leading the opposition between 1989 and his retirement in 2005), and Manley's one-time mentor, Fidel Castro, attended the former leader's Kingston funeral in 1997. Seaga, who also attended (and spoke at) Marley's funeral, paid silent tribute to his old enemy as he stood quietly, head bowed, beside his coffin with none of their one-time bitter rivalry evident.

"IT IS NOT ME SAYING THESE THINGS, IT'S GOD.. IF GOD HADN'T GIVEN ME A SONG TO SING, I WOULDN'T HAVE A SONG TO SING."
BOB MARLEY

EXODUS

The album's title had been chosen by The Skipper before this title track was written. Exiled in Nassau, Marley equated his forced exit from Jamaica with the departure of the Israelites from Egypt. It was the movement of Jah people out of Babylon and forward to The Promised Land.

Repatriation to his spiritual home remained a big part of Marley's vision until he passed on. "Today is not the day," he said in 1976, "but when it happen, 144,000 of us go home." Twelve tribes of 12,000 – Reuben, Simeon, Levi, Judah, Issachar, Zebulun, Dan, Gad, Asher, Naphtali, Joseph and Benjamin – all going home to Zion. (The reggae star himself was, because of his February birth, a member of the tribe of Joseph, and was believed by some people, including Judy Mowatt, to be a reincarnation of Joseph himself).

'Exodus' was hailed by Marley's label as the first single to be picked up by black radio stations in North America, and the Caribbean's star's US audiences began to reflect this breakthrough. By the late Seventies, his audiences had broadened beyond the hip (and in many cases well-off) whites who had been with him from the beginning, to the urban black community he had long wooed without being noticed.

Like other great songwriters, Marley saw himself only as a conduit, channelling the word of Jah to the masses: "It is not me saying these

BOB MARLEY
WITH MANAGER
DON TAYLOR.

things, it's God," he declared. "If God hadn't given me a song to sing, I wouldn't have a song to sing."

GUILTINESS

When he was working in the studio, Bob Marley spoke little (and laughed even less), but communicated constantly with the other musicians through facial expressions and body movements.

By the time the *Exodus* album was recorded, Marley and his Wailers had developed a tight musical rapport, and before any Wailers' song was recorded it had been rehearsed so often that few takes were required. Everyone associated with Bob Marley – engineers, musicians, family, friends, manager, label executives – all talk of his endless discipline and devotion to rehearsal.

"He was a perfectionist," Breakespeare notes, a view echoed by Chris Blackwell, Don Taylor and many others. Marley's take on his work habits was simple: "I have a job to do and want to do it well."

'Guiltiness' is not one of the reggae icon's better-known compositions. Its admonition to the "downpressors" (Rasta-speak for "oppressors"), the "big fish who always try to eat... the small fish" is a truism that is, in the Jamaican experience, timeless. The slave masters have merely been replaced by an even more insidious system that imprisons the poor as effectively as the strongest iron chains.

The *Exodus* album contains many references to guilt and innocence and the confusion between the two. It is a truism that the island's justice system, despite being based on British law, is heavily biased against the poor, and that "guilty until proven innocent" is the maxim that guides most arrests (or killings) of not only ghetto residents, but anyone who doesn't have friends in high places.

THE HEATHEN

Even before the advent of Rastafari, Jamaica was one of the most devout nations on the planet, its enormous number of churches competing only – somewhat ironically – with its equally impressive number of bars. Still the heathen would flourish. Like nowhere else on earth, good and evil are in constant battle for control of this beautiful isle. And it is this duality in the national character that gives Jamaica its sometimes dangerous, and deadly fascinating edge, setting up a creative tension that so often is stretched beyond normal breaking point, but, for reasons unknown, never actually snaps.

To be called "heathen" in Jamaica is as bad as, or worse than, being called a "batty man" (gay). Society's rules are simple and all too often based on a very literal interpretation of the Bible's Old Testament. People are regularly stoned, chopped or beaten to death for crimes that in other societies would be dealt with legally and with far less severity, like theft. Heathens, whether real or imagined, are not so drastically disposed of, but they are shunned by all.

Perhaps fittingly, given a tendency in Jamaica to view rock music suspiciously, 'The Heathen' is the song on *Exodus* that has the most rock guitar on it. Junior Marvin gives the track an almost ominous feel, which reinforces Marley's lyrics quite effectively.

Pretty women and potent herb were as important to Robert Nesta Marley as politics and his quest for local – and world – peace. In this context, *Kaya* is as valid an album as *Survival,* but Marley was more than ready for the mixed response: "Too much romance with Miss Breakespeare," he laughed to Cindy, "ca' me is a militant yout'." But, regardless of the controversy, *Kaya* went to Number 4 in the UK charts during the week of its release. And Chris Blackwell says that *Kaya* is his favourite album, because, he says quite simply, "it's full of joy."

This complimentary assessment of the controversial album contrasts sharply with Don Taylor's assertion that Blackwell didn't intend to put the album out because it was too "soft" (a catch-all Jamaican phrase for anything that isn't happening).

In addition to its local significance, the One Love concert was thought of as an appropriate, if unofficial, opening date for The Wailers' first world tour, which, after their usual successful swing through Europe, produced another live album. The double LP set, *Babylon By Bus,* took its title from a review written in London's influential music rag, the *New Musical Express.*

THE *ONE LOVE* PEACE CONCERT IN KINGSTON WHERE MARLEY JOINED THE WARRING HANDS OF MANLEY AND EDWARD SEAGA.

103

Capturing the extraordinary energy that had left European fans on a great high, *Babylon By Bus* contained tracks like 'Lively Up Yourself' (which had also appeared on *Live!*), 'Is This Love', 'No More Trouble', 'Positive Vibration' and 'Punky Reggae Party'.

'Punky Reggae Party' had been recorded in London's Hammersmith studio in the early summer of 1977 for Lee "Scratch" Perry. This was the year that punk rock was emerging as England's dominant music force, and although initially skeptical about its message, Marley – appreciative of punk's use of reggae rhythm – soon embraced the music's rebellious stance. Taking his cue from groups like The Clash (last seen in Jamaica in 1982 wearing very un-punk-like woven palm leaf hats, decorated with bobbing birds) he began to incorporate a little of punk's outrageous attitude into his own work. "In a way," he said, "me like to see dem safety pins an't'ing. Me nah do it miself, but mi like see a man can suffer without crying."

At the session was the three-man British reggae group, Aswad (Brinsley Forde, Tony Gad, and Drummer Zeb), Cat Coore on guitar and Ibo Cooper on organ. Perry that day was "jumping around the studio, doing little dances and all of a sudden creating parts which separately made no sense, but which came together in a kind of counter-melody marriage.

THE CLASH, A BAND WHOSE MUSIC OWED MUCH TO THE INFLUENCE OF REGGAE.

"MAYBE IF I'D TRIED TO MAKE AN ALBUM HEAVIER THAN KAYA, THEY'D HAVE ASSASSINATED ME."
BOB MARLEY

Perry weaves a very good tapestry. As for Bob Marley, Cooper – himself an inspiration to many – describes him as "very inspiring… he went nine hours with neither spliff nor food. He just stayed in the (vocal) booth and kept on singing." At the end of these nine long hours, Perry went home with two outstanding tracks: 'Punky Reggae Party' and 'Keep On Moving'. Both of these songs were to become staples of the singer's live shows.

With Europe done and *Babylon By Bus* out and selling, the next focus was the United States, and after some initial problems getting Junior Marvin into the country because of an old drugs charge, the tour got off to a slightly-delayed start on May 19, 1978 in Cleveland, Ohio.

The tour arrived in Toronto, Canada, on a balmy Friday night on June 9, Marley playing the famous, and recently closed, 20,000-seater Maple Leaf Gardens, and the audience, a mixed bag of black and white united under a sea of red, green and gold tams, T-shirts, scarves, buttons and beads, was as responsive to Marley's hypnotic music as if born to the one-drop beat. When Bob said, "Jah!", the crowd roared "Rastafari", and when the concert ended and hundreds of people boarded the northbound subway car at Yonge and College, an impromptu passenger version of 'One Love' carried the train not to its intended destination of Finch Avenue, but, instead, straight to Zion.

When the tour reached Madison Square Gardens, the *New York Times* critic hailed the sold-out concert as "a triumph… for reggae in general, and for Mr Marley in particular." A few months later, Marley was honoured in New York by the United Nations which presented him with a Medal of Peace.

Following the last date in America, Marley briefly returned to Jamaica, linking up with his longtime producer and friend, Scratch Perry for a short studio session during which he recorded four songs. Island's reggae star was able to do this because, as the first Jamaican artist to enjoy a properly negotiated contract, he had retained "Caribbean rights", or the right to record himself, or for other producers, and to distribute any such Wailers material throughout that territory on his own label. It was a way of not only controlling the group's output in their own region, but also of maintaining a critical presence in their home market.

Marley was glad of his short respite "back a yard". Ahead was The Wailers' first tour of Australia, New Zealand and the Far East. No one was sure how this group of serious-looking musical messengers from Jamaica, the first reggae act ever to perform on such alien shores, would be received. As it turned out, no one need have worried. When The Wailers' plane, running one-and-a-half hours late, touched down in Sydney at about 11:00pm on a damp and drizzly night, the Aussies were eager to welcome the band to a new and appreciative audience down under. And in both Australia and New Zealand (particularly the latter) the group's usual white fans were joined by the continent's indigenous inhabitants who, in Auckland, met Marley's plane and bestowed upon him a native name meaning "redeemer". These native people gravitated naturally to The Wailers music (as indeed the Hopi Indians would in the United States) as though it was meant for them.

Japan was equally receptive to reggae's alluring beat and its seductive leader (although not at all receptive to the weed that went with it, a restriction that Don Taylor had to get around by carrying his client's supply into the country in his shoes). It was an interest in Jamaica and its music that was to grow steadily from this first introduction in 1978 and would last until the mid-Nineties when it died off during the dancehall-induced stagnation of Jamaica's once unstoppable music production.

SOCCER PLAYER ALAN 'SKILL' COLE, MARLEY'S FRIEND AND CONFIDANTE.

But back in the late Seventies, no music was newer and more exciting than reggae and the excitement generated at The Wailers' Tokyo show lit a spark that led thousands of young Japanese fans on a pilgrimage to the Caribbean island home of Robert Nesta Marley, some of whom would stay on, living and working with the people and learning patois – all the better they would shyly admit "to understand what Bob Marley say".

After a couple of other stops – including Hawaii – the 1978 tour ended in Nassau. With the end in sight, the tired Wailers could take great satisfaction in having taken their music right around a globe that was still skanking in the tour's wake.

The final significant event of this busy year was that Robert Marley – following his friend Skill Cole, who had left Jamaica for Ethiopia in 1996 – made what for him was a holy pilgrimage, his very first visit to the African continent. Although he, and manager Don Taylor who had accompanied him, reportedly stayed in Ethiopia with Skill Cole for only four days (the same length of time that Haile Selassie spent in Jamaica), the visit actually reinforced Marley's Rastafarian belief in repatriation, and inspired some of his best work, including 'Zimbabwe', as well as, says Taylor, a plan to one day build a $4 million settlement for the Rastas resident in Ethiopia.

TIME WILL TELL

Family Man Barrett says 'Time Will Tell' was written by "me an' Bob in Nassau", where the band had gone to escape further attacks on Marley's life. The most serious song in the *Kaya* collection came about during a makeshift session in Chris Blackwell's house. "We set up the drums and a tape machine... I was the engineer," says Barrett," and between us the lyrics and music came together."

The "strange acoustic piano" at the beginning of the song sets its mood, and is, says drummer Barrett, him playing keyboards while "imagining how Fats Domino would do it." Barrett also says that many of the quirky little keyboard parts heard on other songs were also his. "Sometimes, as arranger, I used to add to Tyrone's keys."

Time Will Tell' boasts one of the best remembered of Bob Marley's lines, "Think you're in heaven but you're really in hell", a perfect allegory for the two sides of Jamaica. From the pretend paradise of the island's idyllic northcoast to the grim nightmare of the ghetto, heaven and hell, had, by the late Seventies, become interchangeable. As for the main message of the song, it was a warning meant not for the gunmen "who run come crucify the dread", but for the powerful "baldheads" who "set them up".

Released as it was in 1978, time was already telling. The border of the political war zones of Kingston's inner city were becoming blurred in a cloud of shared ganja smoke. Beginning to see the senselessness of politically encouraged slaughter, the opposing factions of the ghetto had begun to reason. A peace council had been established, and it was as part of this movement that the One Love Peace Concert had been organized. But, as soon as an informal truce had been called, it began to fall apart. Peace was the last thing the politicians actually wanted.

IS THIS LOVE?

One of the two songs on *Kaya* which charted 'Satisfy My Soul' being the other one 'Is This Love?' is one of those enduring love songs that is covered endlessly in Jamaica by northcoast hotel bands whose target audience is

"THINK YOU'RE IN HEAVEN BUT YOU'RE REALLY IN HELL."
BOB MARLEY

107

the steady flow of casual, mixed-colour couples who meet and make out probably on a single hotel bed. And it was one of the main songs in the repertoire of a magical band called Happiness Unlimited (resident band at the Intercontinental Hotel in Ocho Rios in 1981), that convinced Stevie Wonder first to jam with them, then to sign them, and finally to take them back to LA.

If the central inspiration was Cindy Breakespeare, then the story begins with their meeting. "We met at 56 Hope Road," she says. "I was renting an apartment downstairs (from Chris Blackwell) and lived there with my brother. Bob (by then her new landlord) and me kept passing each other in the garden. One day he stopped to talk, and that was it." Still a teenager, Breakespeare says that she was at an age when "attachments come easily". Yet she knew instinctively that this flirtation was different: "I said to myself, get involved with this dude and he'll change your life for ever." Don Taylor says he knew something was afoot when "Cindy stopped paying rent," and maintains that Breakespeare was not only the true love of Bob Marley's life, but the only woman he respected.

In Jamaica, beauty queens (especially Miss Worlds) are afforded a much higher social status than musicians (no matter how famous), and Breakespeare, used as she was to the social mores of uptown, admits that Marley's expectations required some consideration. "I had to ask myself if I was ready to throw away my razor and nail polish – Bob lived his Rasta philosophy and liked his women natural."

KAYA

'Kaya' was one of the songs originally recorded for Scratch Perry who later did a dub version of the tune for his *Soul Revolution II* (an album released in Jamaica as a limited edition and now very rare). Seventeen-year-old Steven Stanley was the engineer for the dub session which was held in late February, 1978, at the Chin Loy-owned Aquarius Studio in Kingston's Half Way Tree. "Bob," he says, "let Scratch control everything... he was mostly in the back smoking, he didn't say much at all." Marley, who, after the 1976 attempt to take his life no longer liked to travel alone in Jamaica, arrived at Aquarius (dressed as usual "in a jeans suit") with his political posse in this instance, Claudie Massop, Bucky Marshall and a few other people who were, in Stanley's words, "nevah too right".

The Aquarius session lasted all day and not once did Marley inject himself into the mix. Scratch didn't know the board (Aquarius was the first studio in Jamaica to offer a 24-track board – a Rosser custom-built model) so he had Stanley balance and then "punched in and out to get whatever dub effect he wanted", relates the renowned Stanley, who then tells an interesting post-session story of being driven home by Claudie Massop in the JLP don's black BMW and getting stopped en route by police who started to search the car. "When someone on the street tell the police is who," Stanley laughs, "dem stop search and tell Claudie dem jus' a pull 'im leg."

No longer a popular term for weed, the word "kaya" has been redefined as a Marley album title. This song is saying that it was herb that got The Skipper (whose favourite type of herb was lamsbread or Jerusalembread – aka goatshit) through a lot of rainy days – the term outlasts definitions.

SATISFY MY SOUL

Bob Marley liked to do new versions of his old songs and many of the tracks featured on The Wailers' ten Island albums were first recorded as singles for early producers like Scratch Perry. 'Satisfy My Soul' was originally done for Perry (when it was known as 'Don't Rock The Boat' as well as 'I Like It Like This').

With this new version, Marley took back the publishing rights. But it is now believed that Perry did contribute to the writing of some of the Wailer songs he produced.

EE 'SCRATCH' PERRY, A LEGEND IN HIS OWN TIME (NOT TO MENTION HIS MIND).

SUN IS SHINING

'Sun Is Shining', another *Kaya* track first produced by Lee Scratch Perry and released as 'To The Rescue', was written in Wilmington, Delaware, when Marley was living with his mother and doing one of several menial jobs he held under the pseudonym, Donald Marley.

From *Kaya*'s reference to "rain is falling", this song offers a rather more optimistic take on life, and where ganja got him through the rain, memories of the morning sun – a powerful and positive reminder of Jamaica's blessings – kept him going through a numbing week of work in a cold country far from home.

Arguably the best-mixed track on the album, Chris Blackwell and Robert Ash also created a haunting, dub-enhanced version of a song that is best listened to while driving in a convertible with the top down along Jamaica's comely coastline, on one of those lazy, lovely days that really can make Jamaica seem like Eden.

The recording of 'Sun Is Shining' followed much the same pattern as most of Island's Bob Marley And The Wailers catalogue. In the early days when they were still recording in Jamaica, The Wailers would start with an acoustic guitar, a rhythm box and a scratch vocal, before laying down four "bed" tracks – drums, bass, piano and rhythm guitar. By the time they had switched their main recording venue to the UK, the basic rhythm tracks had expanded from four to ten or more. They added more drums, percussion and lead guitar, and from *Kaya* on, horns as well.

'Sun Is Shining' has proved an enduringly popular track. In 1999, Danish house producer Martin Otteson earned himself the distinction of being the first remixer to receive official clearance from the Marley Estate. His reworking of the song, featuring Marley's vocals backed by a gentle house beat, was an unexpectedly huge international hit. Credited to "Bob Marley vs. Funkstar de Luxe" the remix topped the US dance charts and was a top three single in the UK.

EASY SKANKING

For the uninitiated, skanking is a slow dance best done when stoned. And for a time, in the late Seventies, it seemed like the whole island was skanking in steady and sensual unison. The spoilers of this enchanted and surprisingly – despite the endemic violence – innocent world, were the police, who had orders to stop-search, prosecute and then ask questions later.

"BOB WAS MOSTLY IN THE BACK SMOKING. HE DIDN'T SAY MUCH AT ALL... HE JUST KEPT SMOKING." **STEVEN STANLEY, ENGINEER**

As the decade neared its end, the Rastafarian movement, with its primary focus on peace, was, for a country controlled by tribal warfare, getting alarmingly strong, and efforts by authorities to undermine Rasta culture intensified. Roadblocks, manned by both police and M-16-toting soldiers, were found everywhere on the island, and "possession" was interpreted on the scene.

Many reggae artists including Bob Marley ignored the danger of open smoking (Peter Tosh going to jail for his defiance). But, unlike Tosh whose natural tendency was to taunt, Marley was subtle. "Excuse me while I light my spliff" was his gentle way of telling Babylon to go to hell.

MISTY MORNING

The island of Jamaica is most beautiful and most addictive – on misty Blue Mountain mornings when you "don't see no sun", but the mist is a comforting buffer between you and the real world that is slowly waking up around you.

'Misty Morning' was written by a homesick Marley while he was in Delaware toiling for the money which he eventually used to start his own small label. He was later to say that he missed waking up in Jamaica – missed the feeling of knowing you're "back a yard" as the night croak of the tree frogs gives way to the ubiquitous cock crowing that heralds the start of every Jamaican day.

He also missed Cindy Breakespeare, who ended up living with him at various times while he was recording in London. Of time spent with him in the studio, she says that she was merely "like a fly on the wall". When Marley was working he only had time for his music.

SHE'S GONE

Not many women left Bob Marley. He, not she, was the one who would usually be gone. And Marley's celebrity and wealth guaranteed that there was always another pretty woman waiting patiently in the wings.

For a man who considered marriage a trap, it is likely that lines in the song like "she felt like a prisoner that needs to be free" told more about him than any of his "plenty women". And although he and wife Rita were leading separate lives for many years before his death, Rita Marley's amazing tolerance makes Hilary Clinton's staying power look tame. Asked just after what would have been her husband's 54th birthday how her

husband's lasting infidelity had affected her, Rita's reply to the Jamaican entertainment reporter was stoical but honest: "I am a normal woman and things can happen that depress you."

The musical arrangement of 'She's Gone' harkens back to the Sixties sound of Jamaica. The echo chamber effect on the vocal is a throwback to early toasters like URoy and Errol Scorcher, and gives the words a plaintive resonance that communicates pain – whether it's his or hers is a question that will never be answered.

RUNNING AWAY

One of the most simple and most powerful of Marley's songs, 'Running Away', said to be written about his 18 months in exile, can be interpreted on many different levels. Of the shooting, Marley would say (in February, 1978) that he "knew something was going to happen". He had, he said, a "vision" (prophetic dream) of being in a barrage of gun-shot". Knowing when he woke up that this premonition was serious, he talked about it

*"ME NAH RUN,
SO ME HAFE STAY
SAFE AND NOT
RUN."*

**BOB MARLEY, ON
THE HOPE STREET
SHOOTING**

with his "bredren", mentioning that the message of his vision was that he shouldn't run. When vision became reality and he heard the first gunshots at 56 Hope Road, his first thought was to run but, flashing back to the dream, he remembered that in vision "me nah run, so me hafe stay and not run."

Not fleeing from the gunfire saved his life. But by leaving the island shortly thereafter, first for Nassau and then for London, he was still running, living, in a sense, like his would-be murderers, on the lam. He realized then that the one impenetrable obstacle to real escape – whether from actions or feared consequences – was one's self.

CRISIS

Marley's fatalistic belief of "I knew I was born with a price on my head," gave his music a great deal of its edge. He had just completed the recording of 'Crisis' before travelling back to a country that, in the wake of Michael Manley's misguided courting of Cuba, was facing the worst crisis in its history. The politicians' plan of divide and plunder, which had worked so well for so long, was now backfiring big-time as the people started to march to the radical Rasta drummer, and the downtown dons were uniting in a common people's cause. Tellingly, the People's National Party's minister of national security (called in the current crisis the "minister of national insecurity") denounced the peace effort.

The event that precipitated the peace initiative was the Green Bay Massacre, when ten gang members of the Jamaica Labour Party (the party in opposition to the PNP) were shot by the Army. Five men died. Five survived and escaped. Some thought that Manley had set it up. Others accused opposition leader Edward Seaga. But whoever was behind the slaughter, the clear message to the rival gangs was that they were all expendable pawns in the game. This was the changing order that faced Marley on his return to Jamaica.

In the 'Crisis' mix, Chris Blackwell and Robert Ash captured the tension of those dangerous days, the instruments, at times, hovering like the helicopters despatched (unsuccessfully) to find the Green Bay survivors, before coming back together in the irie groove that marked the best of Marley's work. Speaking to Blackwell about this, he remembers the day that Marley did the final vocal. "I told Bob about changing 'Crisis'. There was one part that didn't work as well as the rest. He kind of grunted, but then put in a new piece instantly."

1979

PRODUCED BY BOB MARLEY
AND THE WAILERS AND ALEX
SADKIN

SURVIVAL

With a theme of African solidarity, reinforced by a Neville Garrick-designed jacket of many flags, *Survival*, the ninth of the ten albums contracted by Island Records, was released in the late summer of 1979, the Jamaican version coming out on clear vinyl with typeface in red, green and gold. Co-produced by Bob Marley And The Wailers and English engineer, Alex Sadkin (who would die in a Caribbean car accident a few years later), the album was recorded in London at Island's Basing Street Studio.

In Jamaica, things were dread. The economy had come to a standstill and the country was bankrupt. Michael Manley's vision had failed and he was now viewed more sinner than saviour. People began to predict that Manley would lose in the following year's election.

Despite attempts to portray him as a People's National Party supporter, Robert Nesta befriended the "top rankin'" of both parties, and would never acknowledge any affiliation to anything other than the "Rastafarian party". As he expressed it: "Only one government me love, the government of Rastafari."

Marley had far less difficulty aligning himself with political causes overseas, and accepted eagerly when invited to perform at the midnight ceremony held at Rufano Stadium in Salisbury (soon to be Harare) to mark the handing over of Rhodesia by the British to the Africans as the new state of Zimbabwe on April 18, 1980. "Natty gonna mash it inna Zimbabwe", he sang. And he did. Thousands of Africans wildly cheered the slight figure on as he delivered his tribute to the newly-liberated nation.

'Zimbabwe', the song that defined the independence celebration (and which appears on the *Survival* album), was not, as is commonly thought, written for the occasion. Rather, it was composed the year before in Shashamani, Ethiopia, on Marley's first visit to the African continent. Shashamani is a Rastafarian settlement built by the first (and almost the last) of the Jamaican

Rastas who emigrated to Ethiopia not only believing that the ultimate goal of all Selassie I's followers was repatriation to the homeland, but having the pioneering courage to act on their belief.

Not only 'Zimbabwe' but several of the other songs on *Survival* had their origins in Shashamani. As early as 1974, Marley had verbalized his desire to "go to Africa and write some music", and when he finally "reached" – after, according to Don Taylor who was with him, two unexplained denials of his visa application by Ethiopian officials, before a third accompanied by cash was successful – the creativity flowed almost non-stop.

Co-producer Alex Sadkin, who had first worked with Bob Marley as an engineer on *Rastaman Vibration*, had been hired for the *Survival* sessions by Chris Blackwell. Although, in an interview, manager Don Taylor dismisses Sadkin as "one of Chris Blackwell's white flunkies", he describes him in his book, Marley And Me, as a Bob Marley find who was later lured into the Island fold. But, however he came to be involved, Alex Sadkin has always had a good reputation in reggae circles and is recognized as a legitimate contributor to the music and its international success. *Survival* is the only one of the ten albums recorded for Island Records that Chris Blackwell "had nothing at all to do with". Sadkin and Marley had full control over the production. Yet, it contains Blackwell's favourite song – 'So Much Trouble In The World', a track he singles out for both its faultless content and production.

Survival is unusual in that it left no room at all for love songs. Its purpose was 100 per cent political, and was probably an attempt to balance the "soft" content of *Kaya*, and to silence the hardcore critics of his last studio album.

The title of the album spoke not only of his own narrow escape from death, and to the reversal of the black Diaspora, but would also find a resonance back home where the basic survival of the people of Jamaica into the next decade was in grave jeopardy. Supermarket shelves were bare, candles were a common option to a patchy supply of electricity, and cheques written by the government to pay the nation's bills were bouncing with alarming regularity. Manley's sweet socialist dream had now turned into a bitter nightmare of mammoth proportions.

In July of 1979, Bob Marley And The Wailers were booked to headline Reggae Sunsplash, the second year of a festival started in Kingston that grew in a new venue in Montego Bay to be one of the biggest events in the reggae year – until a string of bad business decisions resulted in the collapse of the original format and the demise of the Sunsplash vibe.

"IN A WORLD THAT FORCES LIFELONG INSECURITY… WE'RE THE SURVIVORS."
BOB MARLEY

The thousands of reggae addicts who would make the annual trek from as far afield as Japan and Siberia come no more, and the parks that once resounded to the driving drum and bass beat for four days and nights are now silent. No more all-night sessions, no more complaining about long band changes, or of the bathroom attendants charging JA$1 per sheet of toilet paper. No more trying to sleep under the stage on "reggae beds" (sheets of cardboard that were sold for JA$50), and no more staggering home and feeling like you wanted to sleep for a week. But then going back and doing it all over the following year.

The night that Marley played, it had been raining, and Sunsplash when it rained was a nightmare of mud, in parts six inches deep. There were no changing rooms for artists, or even a decent shelter backstage. The artists would arrive in minibuses, pull up to the side of the stage, and when announced, run up the high wooden stairs and straight into the spotlight. On this particular night, the mud was so bad it even made it onto the stage and Marley joked about it as he launched into 'Lively Up Yourself', before previewing songs from *Survival*. As a continuous spiral of suspicious smoke drifted high above the crowd of 15,000, and moved slowly across the lights beamed from the back of the park, no one remembered the rain or the mud any more. Marley was burnin' "on the box" – nothing else mattered.

ZIMBABWEANS TOOK TO THE STREETS TO CELEBRATE THEIR INDEPENDENCE IN 1980 – BOB MARLEY PERFORMED AT THE MIDNIGHT CEREMONY.

117

In September, Marley did another show in Jamaica – this one at Kingston's National Arena, a benefit for children. Again, he tried out a couple of his new tunes, but for the children, the fun started when he sang the songs that every child in Jamaica could sing the chorus to.

It was hard for Marley to stay in Jamaica during the long dark days of the late Seventies. People were selling out and leaving the island by the thousands, choosing the uncertainty of a new country and the difficulties imposed by the US$50 limit on funds that could be taken with them (all additional funds had to be left in the island), over the known hardship of Jamaica where the luxury houses they were leaving behind were fetching US$30,000 at best. A bumper sticker popular at the time read, "Will the last person to leave Jamaica please turn off the lights."

Ironically, by the end of 1979, every one of the political heavyweights who had been involved in the peace truce of the preceding year was dead. Claudie Massop and Bucky Marshall were gunned down, and Byah Mitchell died from a cocaine overdose.

BABYLON SYSTEM

In its widest interpretation, "Babylon" is the world system (or "Shitstem" as Peter Tosh called it) of inequality and injustice. In its narrowest sense it is "the vampire sucking the blood of the sufferah" – the Jamaican police. The Jamaican Constabulary Force has never had the trust or respect of the island's people, especially not that of the poor whose basic human rights have too often been blatantly ignored. Intimidated and abused (and sometimes, reportedly, even killed) more than they have been "served and protected", it is not hard to understand their reluctance to trust. With this "us" against "them" tradition, Bob Marley's words found thousands of ready ears. Everyone in the ghetto, and more than a few of his uptown followers, were willing to fight to right the wrongs of Babylon.

"Babylon is everywhere. You have wrong, and you have right. Wrong is what we call Babylon…" said Marley, who liked to boast of his ability to explain things in terms simple enough for a baby to understand, and who saw his own birth to a "white man of war" (as he once described his father) and a simple, unsullied, black country lass, as a personal example of Babylon's reach. He also cautioned against the indiscriminate use of the term by those who didn't properly understand it, explaining that, "a certain word can hold you out from the truth a long while… so (you) become an idiot (you) become more chained, 'cause a thing is right or wrong…

if you're right you're right an' if you're wrong you're wrong". Put more metaphorically in the song as "you've been trodding on the wine press much too long", he had a simple answer: "Babylon no wan' peace. Babylon wan' power."

One of the key weapons of Marley's war against the wrongs of Babylon, and one of the most popular of his ideas, was the smoking of herb as the answer to, if not everything, at least a great deal. "The more people smoke herb, the more Babylon fall," he promised. Rasta promoted weed as the "healing of the nation", but also as the conveyer of truth to troubled, rebellious minds. To ensure his own access to the "truth", Marley, says Don Taylor, was the only rock star to have the "provision and supply of marijuana written into his contracts".

AMBUSH IN THE NIGHT

After the night ambush in December, 1976, Bob Marley left Jamaica in a chartered jet for the Bahamas and went into hiding for several weeks at Chris Blackwell's house in Nassau, before touring up in London to start work on the Exodus album in early 1977. He would not return to Jamaica until February, 1978.

His assailants, Marley said, were known to him, adding that their identity was "top secret". Although his attackers were never brought to legal justice, three of the gunmen, says Don Taylor, got stark and swift ghetto justice in June, 1978, when he and Bob were summoned as "witnesses for the prosecution" and taken to a lonely spot by the McGregor gully. He then recounts how one of the three confessed to being trained as an agent by the CIA and given unlimited supplies of guns and cocaine to ensure their cooperation in carrying out orders to kill the man who was being increasingly seen as a threat by those who had a vested interest in keeping the political "runnings" just the way they were.

The gunmen pleaded for mercy but to no avail. Two were taken away and hanged. The third was shot in the head. A fourth suspect, never apprehended by either justice system, was said to have self-destructed on cocaine. The most compelling part of Taylor's story is his description of how a "ghetto general" offered the gun to Marley, giving him the chance to personally execute his enemy. "Marley," says Taylor, with no hint of emotion, "declined the offer."

Ultimately, Marley's take on the Hope Road shooting was that it was a "good" experience. And "nobody died".

AFRICA UNITE

REGGAE'S MESSIAH
PERFORMING ONE OF
HIS MOST POLITICAL
– AND PASSIONATE –
SONGS, THE ROUSING
'AFRICA UNITE'.

Reggae's Messiah stated on many occasions that his message was for the whole world, but his heart was Africa. More than anything, he said, his dream would be realized with the reunification of the separated states of his ancestral homeland. Nearly 20 years after his death, it is Europe that has united, and, apart from a slowly-growing recognition of commonality between US and Caribbean blacks, Africa and its peoples are as divided as ever. One of the most frustrating ironies for Marley was that despite his work's Afrocentric focus, it was the white people of the world who were his first followers, and who took his cry for one love, one heart, as a call for unity and understanding within the human race. Blacks, particularly in the US were very slow to respond to reggae, and Bob Marley And The Wailers concerts drew crowds that were 85 per cent caucasian. In an effort to increase his acceptance in the black community, the rebel voice of Jamaica purposely planned that the US leg of the *Survival* tour would open at Harlem's legendary R&B venue, the Apollo Theatre.

To a degree, the ploy worked. The Apollo show was a success, winning a few more converts to the Marley cause, and generating lots of good press within the 'hood. But black radio would remain resistant to Marley's

*"HOW GOOD IT
WILL BE TO SEE
ALL AFRICANS
UNITE."*
FAMILY MAN
BARRETT

message, and to reggae in general. Then, as now, airtime was reserved for R&B (and, later, rap), and with the exception of a few weekly one-hour slots on some urban stations, reggae airplay was nonexistent. It would never have a platform powerful enough to catch on in the ghetto, nor inspire black Americans the way it was intended.

In Africa, Bob Marley was more successful. Even though his visits to that continent were minimal, his impact was quite remarkable.

'Africa Unite' is Family Man Barrett's favourite Wailers' track. "Yeah," he reflects in the slow, measured delivery common to many a Rastaman, "how good and how pleasant it will be before God and man, yeah, to see the unification of all Africans."

TOP RANKIN'

The "top rankin'' in Jamaica are those in control. Usually, the term is used to describe the "dons" of the downtown areas who are divided according to political affiliation, but in the song the reference is clearly to the leaders of Jamaica's political parties, Michael "Joshua" Manley and Edward Seaga.

Divide and control is the political strategy that has governed Jamaica for the past several decades. Like a political patchwork quilt, downtown Kingston is made up of adjoining PNP and JLP zones, each one controlled by its own ghetto government and kept in order by party-issued guns. It is a system that worked well for those in power for many years, and though it has long been common knowledge that the politically-engineered "wars" between rival factions have greatly damaged Jamaica as a nation, no serious attempt has ever been made to stop them, and no artist since Bob Marley has consistently railed against it. "Government sometimes don't like what we say because what we say is too plain," said Marley, well aware of the potential pitfalls of speaking out.

As one who saw how it worked from within (that is, from the PNP-controlled Trench Town), and who was perceptive enough to see through the pretence of the politicians, Robert Nesta Marley's increasing popularity with the people, and the street power of words like "they don't want to see us unite, 'cause all they want us to do is keep on fussing and fighting, I tell you all they want us to do is keep on killing one another", made him a frightening threat to the political and social status quo. "I know I was born with a price on my head," he would say later.

In 1980, the year after 'Top Rankin' was released, there were 800-plus murders. It would go down in this Caribbean nation's history as its most violent to date, a record unbroken until 1998 when over 950 killings occurred. In the intervening 18 years things have changed, but not in a way that anyone – even Bob Marley – could have foreseen. Today, the ghetto dons that once were "employees" of the company, now own it, and the guns that used to be fired by order for political leverage, are now fired in far more self-serving ways. Crossing all of the old political borders, the criminals have brought unity to the communities in a way that puts the future of Kingston – and the island itself – under a very large question mark.

WAKE UP AND LIVE

Never a material man, Bob Marley, according to just about everyone who knew him, practised what he preached. His passionate plea to the people of Jamaica, not to take more than you need from society – not to live for today – has, with hindsight, been interpreted by some of his peers as a self-fulfilling prophecy, since the reasoning behind it was that "tomorrow you (might) bury inna casket". What he's saying in this song is that the only way to protect one's life in Jamaica, is to proceed with caution, and with both eyes fully open.

A recurring theme throughout the *Survival* album, and one that was certainly a natural outcome of the Hope Road shooting, is that of the necessity of losing fantasy and finding – or facing – reality.

The island of Jamaica is a place where fantasy is promoted as reality, and the paradise of the pampered few coexists with the hell of the many. It is also a place where danger lurks around every mountain curve, and every hypocrite's smile, and what you see is never, ever what you get.

SURVIVAL

The album's title track, written from the vantage point of another far less troubled Caribbean island, during his brief exile in Nassau, speaks the truth about a government that bills itself as the "people's party", yet does nothing to stop the suffering endemic to the island's poor. If the government cared, the people wouldn't suffer, sings Marley, convincingly, before intimating in the chorus that black is synonymous with survival.

Part of the euphoria generated in the 1976 election came from Michael Manley's promise to the Jamaican people of a future of self-determination, free at last not only of its colonial past but also its latter-day economic dependence on the US. Jamaica for Jamaicans was how it was sold and, for

a brief time, as long as passionate theory didn't have to be backed up by practice, it worked. Soon, however, the light offered by the people's saviour was dimmed by a dark cloud that covered the island in an unrelenting grip of desperation and hopelessness.

Interviewed in London, Marley reaffirmed his distaste for discussing Jamaica (he had previously expressed concern that doing so could lead to his arrest for treason on his return), but maintained his independent stance, and his commitment to only one political entity – Rasta – and one social goal – "to kill the system".

But, even with no outside assistance the system was effectively killing itself. In 1979, even a loaf of bread was hard to come by, each arrival of the bakery truck bringing with it hordes of people begging for their daily bread. And no one was helping: an ill-advised liaison with Cuba had guaranteed that Manley would be ostracized by the US and thereafter be last in line for International Monetary Fund handouts.

RIDE NATTY RIDE

One of the most enduring images of Rastafari's early days when the whole world seemed bathed in a red, gold and green glow, is that of a free-spirited dread, locks loose and flowing in the wind, sitting astride a high-powered motor cycle, zipping recklessly in and out of heavy Kingston traffic. Alternately, there was the rich Rastaman (by then no longer a contradiction in terms) behind the wheel of a new, black, well-polished BMW (which Marley only bought, he said, because it stood for Bob Marley And The Wailers). Either take was a striking visual reminder of Rasta the rebel, the promise-keeper of the poor, and the bearer of hope for a more righteous and more prosperous tomorrow.

MARLEY'S BMW, WHICH HE BOUGHT, HE CLAIMED, BECAUSE THE LETTERS STOOD FOR "BOB MARLEY AND THE WAILERS".

"Natty Dread" is a slang term for any male who sports dreadlocks, "natty" referring to knotted locks, and "dread" being either a real Rastaman or someone who wears locks only for style. The natty dread of the song is Bob, riding on "no matter what they do... or say". He talks of his survival and, in a broader interpretation, the survival of the Rastaman against the formidable odds of almost total societal rejection. The song ends with what is probably a reference to the fiery destruction

CHRIS BLACKWELL
ON THE PATIO OF HIS
COTTAGE ON THE
HILL IN OCHO RIOS IN
THE MID-EIGHTIES.

of the infamous Jamaican city of Port Royal (known in 1692, the year it disappeared beneath the Caribbean Sea after a massive earthquake, as the wickedest city on earth), that could be construed as equally applicable to Kingston in the twentieth century, and Rasta's apocalyptic vision of its eventual demise.

SO MUCH TROUBLE IN THE WORLD

The word "illusion" appears more than once in the lyrics of *Survival*'s songs. This, coupled with directives like "wake up and live" indicate a deep inner struggle with the widening gap between reality and the fantasy that the decadence of the Studio 54 scenes of the Seventies – all of which had made it down to Jamaica – would make the pain go away. A "million miles from reality", Marley muses. And everyone was. People found it easier to disco the night away than to deal with the truth that morning light revealed. Having survived an attempt on his life, Bob Marley was more than aware of what the real world was about, but he also knew from that experience what survival was all about, too.

In some parts of Jamaica, where shops sell T-shirts emblazoned with the slogan "Jamaica No Problem", it is easy to believe the fantasy of the trouble-free tropical island where pleasure never coexists with pain. The northcoast hotels, many of which exclude any local who doesn't drive a "Bimmer" or a "Benz", promote the tourist dream of never-ending fun amid pretty green palm trees and white sand beaches. The first of the all-inclusive hotels, where real life stops at the security gate, opened in Ocho Rios in 1978, the same year that *Survival* came out.

In contrast to all this pretence, Rastafari was reality. And as its primary spokesman, Marley's mission was to open the eyes of the blind and the ears of the deaf and show them that the only way forward was not to run from trouble, nor hide from the truth, but to face it head on and deal with it. "'Cause first thing," he said, "you cannot be ignorant."

When Chris Blackwell is asked why 'So Much Trouble' is his favourite song, he says, "Because it's a perfect track – the mix, sound, vocal, lyrics and melody are all superb."

ZIMBABWE

Dressed in tight black leather pants and matching vest, Marley sang this song of liberation before a sea of beaming, bopping Zimbabweans, who knowing all the words, sang along with their hero. The decision to appear at the independence celebration had been made spontaneously, and confirmed only a couple of days before its date. Expenses for the trip were borne not by the new government, but by Bob Marley himself. Denise Mills, Chris Blackwell's long-time PA and confidante, and a woman who could "get through" with anything once she made up her mind to do so, arranged everything (on Bob's orders) from London in, she says in one of her rare conversations about Bob, "only two days". On the Sunday before the Tuesday of the show, Mills joined Bob's entourage when, after coming in from the heat of Kingston that morning, they left London's Heathrow airport on a regularly scheduled BA flight bound for Harare and an official government welcome. For Mills, as used as she was to travelling with The Wailers, the Zimbabwe visit was a surreal affair. The juxtaposition of the precise colonial manners of Rhodesia (which didn't die as quickly as its name), with the raw, rebellious zeal of liberated Zimbabwe created a circus-like atmosphere, where, as she described it, pomp and circumstance gave way to unfettered joy.

Bob Marley And The Wailers went onstage just after the new red, green and gold flag (which had got momentarily tangled at the base of the

PRINCE CHARLES
INFORMALLY
GREETS CROWDS
AT THE HIGHFIELD
TOWNSHIP,
ZIMBABWE,
FOLLOWING
INDEPENDENCE.

flagpole) was finally up and flying and HRH Prince Charles and President Mugabe had taken their seats for the show. The first words spoken to the newly-christened country were "Viva Zimbabwe"; the first song, 'Positive Vibration'. From the outset, the energy of the crowd was explosive and by the time Marley get to 'I Shot The Sheriff' some ten minutes later, any semblance of order was gone. The police, fearing a riot, responded by firing tear gas into the restive crowd, whereupon The Wailers left the stage, only returning when calm was restored.

The "Zimbabwe" sing-a-long closed the show. Marley later commented on how he had felt solidarity with the people. He would also imply that because the song was written the year before Zimbabwe's independence, and "when the song come out it just happen", that prophecy had played a part in it. Describing what for Marley was a momentous event, he said in an interview with journalist Stephen Davis: "We go to the ceremony to play and we watch the whole thing. Watch the British flag go down and the Zimbabwe flag go up… tell you bwoy… we hear alla dem cannon go off, about 40 yard from where we're standin', y'know. You can just imagine that and how we felt."

1980

PRODUCED BY BOB MARLEY AND THE WAILERS

UPRISING

It was during the recording of *Uprising* that Bob Marley started to feel that something was wrong and suspect that the minor toe injury of a few years back had turned into a major problem. But it was too late, and no one could ever have predicted that such a small axe could fell such a mighty tree.

Uprising was recorded at Dynamics, the studio owned by musician Byron Lee and, for a long time, the best in the country. Not that it was pleasant to record there. Located in a bleak and often dangerous industrial area close to the docks and to Trench Town, the studio itself, like all studios "on the rock" sits behind high, locked and security-manned gates and is only accessible to people who have business being there. Everything about Dynamics was, and remains, basic. Even in 1980, in the middle of its heyday, it offered no frills. But The Wailers, as always, were flexible, and as long as the sound was right (Dynamics could deliver that) and the smoke plentiful, "tings aright".

On January 1, 1980, Bob Marley And The Wailers played their first live concert in Africa, a birthday party for the president of Gabon. This performance was significant in several ways. First, Marley met the president's daughter, Pascaline, a woman he was to woo and conquer, and with whom he had one of his last serious affairs. And, second, a dispute over monies paid for the show – Marley reportedly only got $40,000 of a reputed $60,000 fee – led to a parting of the ways with Don Taylor, his manager. Taylor insists that he did nothing wrong, and that "any such accusation was unfounded", and cites as proof of his client's ongoing trust the fact that the majority of Bob's assets "remained in my name until after his death". Even so, he lost his post as manager, an opening soon claimed jointly by Skill Cole and Marley's former manager, Danny Sims.

Back in Jamaica, in February, Bob Marley and his band finished most of the overdubbing on the tracks recorded

MARLEY WITH JUDY MOWATT AND SOME OF THE WAILERS AFTER RECEIVING AN AWARD, CIRCA 1979.

for *Uprising*, following which Marley took the 75-minute flight from Jamdown to visit his mother in Miami, and to cool out for a couple of weeks before going on to Rio for a five-day trip.

While in Brazil, his health was reportedly good and his writing prolific. But two days after he returned to Jamaica, Inner Circle's lead singer, Jacob Miller, who, with Junior Marvin had gone on the Rio trip with Bob, was killed in a car accident in New Kingston, an event that affected Marley deeply.

When, in April, 1980, Bob Marley And The Wailers got the headline spot at the Zimbabwean independence celebrations, it was, remembered Denise Mills, at very short notice. Against great odds she got Bob, the band and the equipment from points A and B to C on time, but it was "all a bit bizarre". After an official government

JACOB MILLER OF INNER CIRCLE – HE WAS KILLED IN A KINGSTON CAR ACCIDENT IN 1980.

welcome, the kind normally reserved for heads of state, and an afternoon courtesy call on President Mugabe at the palace (replete with an acoustic offering of 'No Woman No Cry' by the guest of honour at the palace piano), the actual performance was interrupted by rioting fans (the ones that weren't allowed in).

Tear gas and the Zimbabwe National Liberation Army guerrillas restored order. A second concert was hurriedly arranged for the following night to placate the people: uncounted thousands of whom showed up for the event. Mills, on the surface a rather conventional Englishwoman who lived a very unconventional life, and who was never phased by the worst of problems, rated the trip to Zimbabwe as "very difficult". Though Marley was pleased that he'd helped the new country usher in its future, "everyone", she said "was glad to go home".

By May, *Uprising* had been mixed and what would be The Wailers' last European tour began in Austria. This time around, the band was playing the big venues, like the San Siro Stadium in Milan, Italy. Several of those on the tour speak of the Milan show as the most inspiring that The Wailers ever produced. Engineer Errol Browne, who with Dennis Thomson, was responsible for the sound on the tour, did both the Zimbabwe and the Milan shows and says that the sheer number of people that showed up for the latter concert was, in 1980, astounding. "Not even football had

"I GOT A PAIN IN MY THROAT AND HEAD AND IT'S KILLIN' ME... I'VE NEVAH FELT THIS WAY BEFORE IN MI LIFE."
BOB MARLEY

her husband's head for his funeral. But, in Germany, Marley kept his head covered by a Rasta tam, nursing a new growth of hair underneath.

After a few months had passed, the men (who Bob's mother called "hangers on") left Germany (some of them, according to Mrs Booker, at her insistence, after she and Rita had secretly tape-recorded one of their conversations), leaving three females to care for Bob: mother Cedella, Diane Jobson (his trusted lawyer and close friend), and Denise Mills.

Mills, a short time before her own death, recalled those days as some of the saddest and most traumatic of her life, saying that "as ill as he was, Bob never lost his spirit", nor, she said, did he lose his mental acuity. He knew what was going on and that he had a couple of traitors in his camp. He also knew that Dr Issels' treatment hadn't worked and that it was time to leave Germany. Then, surprisingly, said Mills, given the pair's acrimonious parting several years before, "he said he wanted to see Don Taylor."

Don Taylor was in LA when he got the call from Bob saying that he was leaving the Issels Clinic for Miami and wanted to meet Taylor there. During this conversation, Marley told Taylor that numerous people had been pressuring him to make a Will (a fact confirmed by Mrs Booker). "He told me that he wanted all his money to go to his children," says Taylor, "and that I should make sure they got it." Recognizing "a sense of finality" at the other end of the phone, Taylor made plans to leave for Miami. But, he says, wondering out loud if he let Bob down, he "wouldn't quite make it in time for the meeting".

As Taylor was leaving LA, in Germany, Denise Mills was chartering a Lufthansa jet (at a cost of $90,000) to fly Marley to Miami's Cedars of Lebanon Hospital.

On Saturday, May 9, 1982, Marley, Booker, Mills and Jobson left the rented Bavarian house that had been home for the past few months, and made their way – with Bob on a gurney, attended by two doctors and a nurse, and dressed in new clothes purchased especially for the flight – to the airport and the waiting 747. Mills described the flight as "very quiet, very sad". All seven passengers on that large empty aircraft knew what fate was waiting at the end of the flight.

Two days later, on May 11, 1982, in a small, private suite at Cedars Lebanon, Robert Nesta Marley, after telling his mother not to cry, went home to Zion.

Confrontation, a title that Marley had already decided on while still working on *Uprising*, and his tenth studio album for Island, was released posthumously in 1983.

The narrow, pot-holed road that twists through the hills of the Parish of St Ann to the village of Nine Miles, where Bob Marley was born and now lies forever, seems endless. It's now almost three decades since the day when hundreds of people lined this road, a few of the hundreds of thousands who had stood, solemnly, all across the island, as Marley made his final journey from Kingston back to his birthplace. But nothing much has changed in the tiny hamlet since then. In fact, says one elderly resident whose lined and weathered face appears carved from mahogany, not *that* much has changed since Marley's birth in 1945.

Cedella Booker, a friendly, self-assured, and out-spoken Rastawoman, has built a house and a restaurant beside her son's simple, concrete mausoleum (where he lies facing to the east, and the continent of Africa). Commuting between Jamaica and Miami, Booker tries to spend as much time at Nine Miles as she can, mingling with the steady stream of visitors who make the long trek to this rural retreat from almost every place on the planet.

MARLEY'S MOTHER, CEDELLA MALCOLM MARLEY BOOKER.

On this particular day, she is holding private court on a veranda talking about the plans she has for the restaurant. It is in the midst of many years of wrangling over her son's estate, and she laments the fact that the whole family hasn't come together and says that "they all forgot that it is I who laid the golden egg". She makes bitter reference to the fact that she was almost removed from the Miami house that Bob bought for her because, she maintains, Don Taylor elected to take out a low-interest mortgage and put the cash that could have bought it outright into high-return investments. It was, she confides, Chris Blackwell who came to her rescue and bought the house (not daughter-in-law, Rita). Not surprisingly, her opinion of Blackwell is high.

"He was like a big brother to Bob. Chris is like family to me – the world has to know that."

Drawing on a spliff, she adds that "Chris was ordained by the Almighty (to straighten out the estate). This is a job he must do. I don't know why everyone must fight against him."

The wrought-iron gates to the concrete crypt – which was manually constructed by local builders – are marked by a red, green and gold Rasta flag, and manned by several country dreads. In the first few years after Bob died, visitors could just hang out and "reason" with his Rasta bredren, or pay respect beside The Skip's tomb (which now also contains the body of his half-brother, Anthony, who, at 19, was, she says, shot and killed by an off-duty Miami cop), without time-limit or restriction. Now, a guided tour of the property is mandatory and costs US$10.

The tour includes the tiny, one-room house where Bob was born. Beside the small, metal, single bed, a candle burns.

A photograph of the man who spent his first, and some of his happiest years on earth in this bare, board room, and who later, with wife Rita, would come "back to country to cool out" – and no doubt share "the shelter of (the) single bed" immortalized in 'Is This Love?' – is placed next to the candle.

A short walk from the house, set high on a hill, is the mausoleum. Before entering the modest building, visitors are required to remove their shoes. Inside, the spirit of Jah's highest steppin' soldier envelops those open to its presence.

The tomb itself is covered in burlap (or "crocus" as Jamaicans call it), on which are painted, in "ites" green and gold, the symbols of Rastafari. At the base of the tomb are a variety of personal objects left as offerings by Bob's devoted fans – locks of hair, poems and tiny talismans – and Bob's first box guitar.

"ONE BRIGHT MORNING WHEN MY WORK IS OVER, I WILL FLY AWAY HOME."
BOB MARLEY

GIVE THANKS AND PRAISE

'Give Thanks And Praise' was written in the late Seventies when Bob Marley's Rasta faith was becoming ever more important in his life. In this song, he conveys the depth of his faith to his fans and his belief in Jah's unfailing "guidance and protection" (a common Rasta greeting).

In a New York hotel room, shortly before his death, Bob Marley became a member of the Ethiopian Orthodox Church, and part of the Christian branch of Rastafari. The Ethiopian Church embraces both Jesus and Jah, baldhead and Rasta, and finds no conflict in doing so. Established in Kingston in 1969, at the behest of a group of Rastamen, the order holds that Haile Selassie, as the direct descendant of King Solomon and the Queen of Sheba, was entitled, as the ruler of Ethiopia, to hold the titles, King of Kings, Lord of Lords, Conquering Lion of the Tribe of Judah,

a belief that concurs with Rasta doctrine. Not all Rastafarians concur with the beliefs of the Ethiopian Church, however, and Marley's baptism signalled a break with his Twelve Tribes of Israel bredren.

Ethiopian priests officiated at the May 21st, 1981 funeral of Robert Nesta Marley – as they would also do six years later following the death of Marley's childhood friend and founding Wailer Peter Tosh. (On September 11, 1987 Tosh was murdered by gunmen during an attempted robbery at his home in Jamaica.)

The priests were led by the Archbishop of the Ethiopian Church for the Western Hemisphere. The funeral service for "Berhane Selassie" (Marley's baptismal name) began at Holy Trinity church on Maxfield Avenue at 8:00am and continued at 11:00am at the National Arena, The bare, concrete hall was decorated with red, green and gold bunting, and above the similarly draped, temporary altar was a large banner with the words, "Hon Robert Nesta Marley, OM" (for Order of Merit, Jamaica's highest honour, which was bestowed on the musician shortly before his death). The service itself gave thanks and praise for the remarkable life

THE FUNERAL OF ROBERT NESTA MARLEY WAS HELD ON A SUNNY DAY IN KINGSTON, MAY 21, 1981.

of one of Jamaica's most revered sons – "It was like a jubilee," says Judy Mowatt, one of the I Threes, who sang on many of Bob Marley and The Wailers' classic cuts.

Both the incumbent prime minister, Edward Seaga, and the deposed Michael Manley attended the service. Seaga, paying tribute to Kingston's fallen idol, quoted the old spiritual that Marley had adapted and made his own… "One bright morning when my work is over, I will fly away home."

JUMP NYABINGHI

A Nyabingi (or Nyabinghi) is a Rastafarian gathering. A jump up is a party. Put them together and a good time is had by all. And, as the Rasta movement's unofficial leader, and as someone who knew how to enjoy himself, Marley's joyful and infectious vocal on this track comes close to explaining his timeless appeal.

The first Nyabinghi (originally called a convention) was held in Kingston's infamous ghetto area, Back-O-Wall, in 1958. Scheduled to last for a month, it was organized as an intended early send-off for some 300 Rastas who believed they were about to embark on a mass back-to-Africa journey (which never materialized). The event, consisting as it did

147

RASTAFARIANS, SYMBOLIC RODS IN HAND, FACING UP TO BABYLON.

of dancing, drumming and plenty of smoking around a huge bonfire of old tires, caused some consternation among the city's fathers. Thereafter, Nyabinghis have been held primarily in the hills where the worship of Jah, and the celebration of the holy herb can go on (and on and on and on) undisturbed.

Reggae music lets you dance without a partner. Dancing solo is not only accepted, it is expected. Stoned dreads, skanking happily alone is a sign of a good Nyabinghi, and at reggae concerts it's quite OK to prance through the crowd, or just "hol' your corner", letting the music do with you what it will. As the drums beat, and the chillum pipe is passed through the long night, the Nyabinghi provides a communal affirmation of faith to the usually disparate and disconnected Rasta tribes. Although not known to frequent too many Nyabinghis in the latter part of his life (time constraints alone preventing him), in the early days of his conversion to Rastafari, Bob Marley was known to have been a regular participant.

This song was, according to Island Records, a particular favourite of the singer's. The original tracks were laid down by Marley and Carly Barrett, the only two Wailers who were not temporarily felled by vaccinations (prior to The Wailers' trip to Gabon). 'Jump Nyabinghi', notable for Barrett's innovative hi-hat, was recorded along with an unreleased song, 'Jungle Fever' (referring to the vaccination, not to black/white liaisons as the phrase would later be interpreted).

CHANT DOWN BABYLON

First called 'I Believe in Reggae Music' when penned in a Belgium hotel room while The Wailers were on the Survival tour; 'Chant Down Babylon' starts off on a very radical note with its threat to "burn down Babylon". But then the word "burn" changes to "chant" and the suggestion of violence as a solution dissolves into a benign resolution to the problem. Music is ultimately a stronger agent of change than any other medium – the reason why Marley was such a threat to the establishment.

'Chant Down Babylon' was written for the *Uprising* album, but not included in the chosen ten. By the time it surfaced on *Confrontation*, the once esoteric terms employed to make Marley's points were finding their way into the speech of North Americans. "Babylon" had now become a convenient way to describe anyone in authority. The poet of rebellion had by then been embraced not only by the avant garde of the East and West coasts, but also by middle America.

THE LEGACY

If nothing else, the early, tragic death of a revered musician guarantees immortality and, like Jimi Hendrix, Elvis Presley, and John Lennon before him, Marley's fan base continues to grow in his absence. Since his death in 1981, sales of the Marley catalog have, in the words of Chris Blackwell, "provided a constant revenue stream". The best seller of the posthumous releases is *Legend*, a compilation of some of the best of Marley's music, which has maintained a constant presence on the Billboard Top Pop Catalog chart, and which spent a record-breaking 19 weeks at Number One.

By choice, and in keeping with the Rastafarian refusal to acknowledge death, Bob Marley died intestate. Several people, including lawyer Dianne Jobson and doctor Pee Wee Herman, tried to persuade the dying Wailer to make a Will while he was still in Bavaria at the Issels Clinic, but the more they tried to persuade him to do so, the more the stubborn singer resisted their attempts.

"Nesta was a Rasta who believed in Universal rights and justice. And a Will is material not spiritual," says Mrs Booker. By not directing the disposition of his multi-million dollar "material" estate, Marley precipitated an acrimonious and controversial ten-year battle for the spoils. As his mother put it, "His body wasn't even cold in his tomb before the scavengers began fighting over his worldly goods."

In the beginning, Rita Marley and Jamaica's Mutual Security Bank were appointed co-executors. Marley's widow was later dismissed, however, for forging her late husband's name on numerous documents to transfer ownership to herself. Both she and her US attorneys, Zolt and Steinberg, were then sued for withholding funds totalling US $14 million – this being over and above the funds purportedly paid over by Don Taylor who claims, "everything that was still in my name I signed over to Rita."

THE SPIRIT OF BOB
MARLEY LIVES ON IN
THE 21ST CENTURY.

Other disputes included a lawsuit brought against Mutual Security Bank by three of the 11 infant beneficiaries; a lawsuit against the estate initiated by the Wailers band; the near-eviction of Mother Booker from her estate-owned Miami home; and, a lawsuit against Booker for the recovery of US $500,000.

Cedella Booker talks of the first business meeting after her son's death, and relates how shocked she was when she learned that she was not one of the 12 legal beneficiaries – widow Rita and Bob's nine natural and two adopted offspring. "The mother's portion," relates Booker, "was a puff of breeze... nothing." She walked out of the meeting "disgusted".

It wasn't until 1991 that the sale of the assets of the estate of Robert Nesta Marley (estimated in 1981 to be worth US $30 million) would be resolved in favour of Chris Blackwell's company, Island Logic – interestingly, not a part of Island Records – for a sale price of US $12.5 million. For that amount, Blackwell, with the approval of all the heirs, purchased Marley's song catalog, recording royalties, distribution rights and Jamaican real estate, including 56 Hope Road as well as the Tuff Gong Studio and manufacturing complex on Marcus Garvey Drive. The Blackwell bid was successful (beating out a better offer from MCA for US $15.2 million, and besting his own first offer – approved by the executor but rejected by the UK Privy Council on appeal – of US $8.5 million in 1989) because his main interest, he said, was in making sure that the estate stayed in the family. "I don't want to own it," he said at the time, "I want only to manage the assets. I think I'm the best person for the job." Terms of the deal included the setting up of a Bob Marley Foundation which Blackwell was to manage for a period of ten years after which ownership would revert back to the widow and six of the children – the other five young heirs having settled for a cash payment of US $1 million each. After speculating that his investment would be paid back by the time ten years had elapsed, Blackwell then added: "I just wanted to be a part of something I helped to build up and I didn't want it to disappear in legal fees."

On the day the estate's destiny was finally decided, one newspaper reported that Rastafarian drummers sat outside the Supreme Court of Jamaica on Tower Street beating out the triumphant news that the life's work of the island's most celebrated Rastaman would stay in Jamaica. On that same day, in an uptown hospital, a baby was born to Bob's eldest son, Ziggy. The child was called Justice.

But none of the legal wrangling had stopped the music from playing, nor the royalties from pouring in. Rita Marley, during a telephone interview

"NESTA'S BODY WASN'T EVEN COLD IN HIS TOMB BEFORE THE SCAVENGERS BEGAN FIGHTING OVER HIS WORLDL' GOODS." **CEDELLA BOOKER MARLEY'S MOTHER**

INDEX